Aquinas on
Transubstantiation

Aquinas on Transubstantiation

The Real Presence of Christ in the Eucharist

REINHARD HÜTTER

The Catholic University of America Press

Washington, D.C.

Cataloging-in-Publication Data available
from the Library of Congress
ISBN 978-0-8132-3177-8

Contents

Preface

This small book has grown over the course of numerous years and in the context of many conversations with teachers, friends, and colleagues. I would like to record my thanks especially to Fr. Romanus Cessario, OP, Nancy Heitzenrater Hütter, Fr. Dominic Langevin, OP, Fr. Dominic Legge, OP, Matthew Levering, Bruce D. Marshall, John Martino, and Fr. Thomas Joseph White, OP.

The book has profited greatly from the theological wisdom and profound learning of Fr. Dominic Langevin, OP. Thanks to his expertise as a sacramental theologian, I was able to improve the overall argumentation, introduce important nuances, and correct various mistakes. I am also grateful for the criticisms and recommendations that two anonymous peer reviewers offered. I am grateful to Meghan Duke and David L. Augustine for their very able editorial assistance. Special thanks go to David L. Augustine for compiling the indexes.

I thank the editors of *Nova et Vetera* (English edition) and of the Catholic University of America Press for granting me permission to reprint material that is included here. The core of this opuscule was presented as a keynote lecture at the International Symposium "Aquinas on the Sacraments" at Ave Maria University, Naples, Florida, in February 2007, and published in *Ressourcement Thomism: Sacred Doctrine, the Sacraments, and the Moral Life*, edited by Reinhard Hütter and Matthew Levering (Washington, D.C.: The Catholic University of America Press, 2010), 21–79. The original book chapter as well as this opuscule make use of sections that originally appeared in *Nova et Vetera* (English edition) 7, no. 1 (2009): 175–216.

I dedicate this book in profound gratitude to the Most Reverend Michael F. Burbidge, bishop of the diocese of Arlington and formerly bishop of the diocese of Raleigh, and to the Most Reverend Bernard E. Shlesinger III, auxiliary bishop of the archdiocese of Atlanta and formerly priest of the diocese of Raleigh. I am indebted to both bishops in more ways than words can express.

Abbreviations

WORKS OF ST. THOMAS

In de An.	*In Aristotelis librum de anima commentarium*
In Meta.	*In duodecim libros Metaphysicorum Aristotelis expositio*
In Phys.	*In octo libros Physicorum Aristotelis expositio*
Sent.	*Scriptum super libros Sententiarum magistri Petri Lombardi episcopi Parisiensis*
SCG	*Summa contra Gentiles*
ST	*Summa Theologiae*

OTHER WORKS

Denzinger	*Compendium of Creeds, Definitions, and Declarations on Matters of Faith and Morals* (ed. Hünermann)

There is a mystery, the greatest of all my stories—not that my adored Lord is in the Blessed Sacrament of the Altar—His word has said it, and what is so simple as to take that word, which is the Truth itself?—but that souls of his own creation, whom he gave his Life to save, who are endowed with his choicest gifts in all things else, should remain blind, insensible, and deprived of that light without which every other blessing is unavailing!—and that the ungrateful, stupid, faithless being to whom *He* has given the Free and Bounteous Heavenly gift shall approach his true and Holy Sanctuary, taste the sweetness of His Presence, feed on the bread of angels, the Lord of glory united to the very presence of its Being and become part of itself, yet still remain a groveler in the earth! (my poor, poor soul) is what we too well experience while lost in wonder of his forebearing Mercy, and still more wondering at our own misery in the very center of Blessedness. Jesus, then, *is there*. We can go, receive him, *he is our own*. Were we to pause and think of this thro' Eternity, yet we can only realize it by his conviction: that *he is there* (O heavenly theme!) is as certainly true as that bread naturally taken removes my hunger. So this Bread of Angels removes my pain, my cares, warms, cheers, soothes, contents and renews my whole being. Merciful God, and I do possess you, kindest, dearest Friend, every affection of my nature absorbed in you still is active, nay, perfected in their operations thro' your refining love.

St. Elizabeth Ann Seton, *Journal*, ca. 1809

Introduction

—————— : ——————

The Eucharist ... is ordained to final perfection.
—Thomas Aquinas, *ST* III, q. 65, a. 2[1]

It is absolutely necessary to confess according to Catholic faith that the entire Christ is in this sacrament.
—Thomas Aquinas, *ST* III, q. 76, a. 1[2]

It might not be too much of an exaggeration to claim that in many segments of contemporary Catholic theology, there is a twofold, interrelated, and profound insecurity pertaining to the understanding of the faith, the *intellectus fidei*. The *first* sense of insecurity relates to the nature and task of theology—to be precise, of dogmatic or systematic theology—as well as its correct relationship to three distinct but interrelated points of reference and accountability: the canon of sacred scripture, sacred tradition, and the living magisterium. Indicative of this sense of insecurity and the ensuing lack of clarity was the Congregation for the Doctrine of the Faith's decision to issue the statement *Donum Veritatis* (Instruction on the Ecclesial Vocation of the Theologian) on May 24, 1990, to help "shed light on the mission of theology in the Church" (no. 1). The *second* insecurity plaguing the understanding of the faith pertains to the most central mystery of the faith, the sacrament of the Eucharist and especially Christ's real presence or, more precisely, Christ's *personal presence* by way of his *corporeal presence*. A certain projection of

1

Modernist sacramental theologies onto the teaching of the Second Vatican Council—under the name of conciliar reception—has in many quarters jettisoned the conceptual apparatus of the dogmatic definition of transubstantiation decreed by the Council of Trent. Numerous new interpretations have arisen, most of them trading on various transient postmetaphysical assumptions.[3] What is left is a widespread, albeit mainly soft, agnosticism regarding the principal doctrinal tenets of this most central mystery—a situation most recently addressed by the late Pope John Paul II's last encyclical *Ecclesia de Eucharistia* (2003).

In this somewhat precarious theological situation, I regard it as salutary to move forward by first moving backward, "upstream, and *listening* to the sources."[4] The time has come—indeed, is overdue—to listen again intently to Thomas Aquinas. Such renewed listening to the *doctor communis* serves a twofold *ressourcement*: first, regarding the nature and task of theology and, second, regarding the very core of the *mysterium fidei*, Christ's real, corporeal, and hence personal presence in the sacrament of the Eucharist. For Thomas paradigmatically shows how the nature and task of theology bear immediately upon the mystery of Christ's Eucharistic presence: it is in discursively beholding the mystery of Christ's Eucharistic presence that the nature and task of theology come to a surpassing fruition.

But we must first step back for a moment. For in the eyes of some, over the centuries, too many barrels of ink have already been spilled and too many library shelves filled with tomes by theologians affirming, denying, or qualifying Christ's real presence in the Eucharist. For example, in the sixteenth century the precisely honed and defensively delineated theological definitions of Christ's sacramental presence (including the rejection of the doctrine of Eucharistic sacrifice, as well as of the doctrine of Eucharistic transubstantiation) became the settled identity markers of various Protestant communities—Lutheran, Reformed, Puritan, (Ana)Baptist—and came to serve as warrants for their separation from the Catholic church. This, in turn, affected Catholic theology of the Eucharist. Especially after

0

the Council of Trent, the doctrine of transubstantiation unsurprisingly became a central identity marker of Catholic orthodoxy under the condition of ongoing ecclesial division, religious polemic, and worst of all, protracted wars of religion in Germany, France, England, and Ireland.

In light of the remarkable ecumenical progress that marked the last century—especially since the Second Vatican Council—the situation seems to have improved in unexpected ways. However, a complex set of equally unexpected new problems has arisen. For the tangible ecumenical progress achieved on many levels over the last four decades in Europe and in North America took place within an increasingly and disturbingly postmetaphysical, post-Christian, positivistic, relativistic, and ultimately subject-driven consumer culture with increasing global reach. The combined effects of this cultural shift have shaped the minds and hearts of many Christians in their well-intentioned but premature and ill-informed judgment that the decisive symbolic step of immediate Eucharistic intercommunion is long overdue, a step that would indeed do nothing but accept and cement the status quo of reconciled difference, or rather, reconciled indifference. Such impatient, enthusiastic ecumenism celebrates the indefinite postponement of the question of truth as the end of an already overly prolonged ecumenical effort. Not infrequently, and easily observable, in broad segments of mainline Protestantism, and for that matter also in not a few Catholic circles, this ecumenical impatience is fueled by a remarkable indifference regarding the most central truths of faith and doctrine.

This agnosticism arises in large part from the widespread insecurity and unease regarding the normative guidance that sacred scripture, dogma, the Fathers, and the church's magisterium provide to theology, as well as from a widespread despair that sustained intellectual contemplation, guided by faith, can and will indeed illuminate the truth of the Christian mystery.[5] This situation is undoubtedly exacerbated by the present widespread disparagement of the science of sacred theology and its two integral components, positive and speculative theology. Contemporary theology in general and Catholic theology in particular are distracted and confused by the currently popular dogmas of cultural constructivism and post-metaphysical relativism; by an increasingly habituated hermeneutics of suspicion ceaselessly attempting to unmask authority, tradition, and the "Truth" with a capital "T" as variations of the "will to power"; and by an uncritical accommodation to extraneous if not injurious criteria of academic excellence and productive research imposed by the late-modern secular university. They are, consequently, encumbered by numerous and various self-doubts, as well as self-deceptions about the nature and task of sacred theology.[6] In light of this theologically precarious situation, a conscious reconsideration of the way the *doctor communis* conceived of the task of sacred theology or holy teaching (*sacra doctrina*) seems to me most salutary.

SACRED THEOLOGY—POSITIVE AS WELL AS SPECULATIVE THEOLOGY

What is at stake in such a *ressourcement* is nothing less than the contemporary recovery of what I regard as the two constitutive components of sacred theology (*sacra doctrina*) according to Thomas Aquinas. The first formal act of sacred theology is the ongoing, active reception of the cognitive content of divine revelation (*principia revelata a Deo*) as proposed in sacred scripture, according to the church's understanding. This first formal act of holy teaching (*sacra doctrina*) might properly be circumscribed by the Latin word *positus* and hence by the name "positive theology." The second formal act of sacred theology is the discursive activity of understanding the faith (*intellectus fidei*), later called "speculative theology." In this second formal act of sacred theology, the *intellectus fidei* draws upon created reality as it delivers itself to the human intellect as "what things are," that is, as substances.[7] It is by this second formal act that holy teaching reaches beyond our state as wayfarers. For, guided by the first formal act and, simultaneously, informed by the infused theological virtues of faith, hope, and charity, the second formal act is essentially ordered to the final end of faith: the knowledge of God and the saints (*scientia Dei et beatorum*), in which the *intellectus fidei* already participates inchoately through the theological virtue of faith. Hence, the *intellectus fidei* is increasingly drawn—elevated—by the Holy Spirit to contemplate that knowledge the consummation of which will be the beatific vision itself.[8] In the following, I hope to show that Thomas's doctrine of Eucharistic conversion reflects the integral unity of the positive and the speculative components of sacred theology, a unity in urgent need of recovery in our contemporary intellectual context of theology.

Not a few contemporary systematic and liturgical theologians take the philosophical commitments of late modernity—commitments that are not necessarily consistent but nevertheless connected mainly in Europe with the names of Hume, Kant, Schelling, Hegel, Heidegger, Derrida, and Foucault and in America with the names of Hume, Locke, James, Dewey, and Peirce—as a normative horizon in which and from which to judge what they regard as premodern conceptualizations of the Christian faith. From their vantage point, Thomas's doctrine of Eucharistic transubstantiation appears inextricably entangled in a purportedly medieval cosmological worldview and committed to an allegedly outdated metaphysics. Upon closer inspection, however, it will become clear that it is precisely Thomas's surpassing reception and application of Aristotle's metaphysics and natural philosophy that saves the notion of *substance* from becoming a mere metaphor, which would inevitably lead to the very loss of what the church's dogma intends to maintain.

Thomas's metaphysical contemplation of Eucharistic conversion—precisely as an integral component of sacred theology—provides surpassing intelligibility to the dogma of transubstantiation as defined and circumscribed by the Council of Trent and as continuously taught by the church's magisterium. Thomas's contemplation gestures toward the blinding light of superintelligibility, experienced as the unique darkness that surrounds this sublime mystery of faith.

I submit and will substantiate the thesis that contemporary Catholic dogmatic theology should reclaim, by way of a recovery of sacred theology, the positive as well as the speculative component of its task. In the present precarious intellectual context for Catholic dogmatic theology, what is at stake is nothing other than the intellectual insight into the faith, the *intellectus fidei*.

In his 1998 encyclical *Fides et Ratio*, the late Pope John Paul II indicated quite clearly the direction that such a right enactment of the *intellectus fidei* should take:

> With regard to the *intellectus fidei*, a prime consideration must be that the divine Truth "proposed to us in the Sacred Scriptures and rightly interpreted by the Church's teaching" [Aquinas, *ST* II-II, q. 5, a. 3, ad 2] enjoys an innate intelligibility, so logically consistent that it stands as an authentic body of knowledge. The *intellectus fidei* expounds this truth, not only in grasping the logical and conceptual structure of the propositions, in which the Church's teaching is framed, but also, indeed primarily, in bringing to light the salvific meaning of these propositions for the individual and for humanity.... For its part, *dogmatic theology* must be able to articulate the universal meaning of the mystery of the One and Triune God and of the economy of salvation, both as a narrative and, above all, in the form of argument. (par. 66)

Thomas's unique integration of positive and speculative theology stands in marked contrast to the almost exclusively narrative approaches of the post-Vatican II dogmatic theologies, chiefly informed as well as structured by the economy of salvation (first and foremost the multivolume work *Mysterium salutis*).[9] A fresh consideration of *sacra doctrina* offers a welcome relief from the ensuing antimetaphysical animus and the anti-Scholastic overreaction. For Thomas, in a surpassing way, was able to integrate narrative and argument, or, in other words, positive and speculative theology, into one seamless enterprise of *sacra doctrina*.[10]

METAPHYSICS—PRIVILEGED INSTRUMENT
OF THE *INTELLECTUS FIDEI*

So far so good, many a post-Vatican II theologian might say. However, there is one other ingredient integral to Thomas's way of sub-
stantiating the discursive aspect of *sacra doctrina*—an ingredient considered irretrievably passé by broad late or postmodern theological
and philosophical consensus, and as a subtle and specious Hellenis-
tic attempt to destroy the pure and simple Hebraic essence of Christianity by some, especially Protestant theologians. This ingredient
is metaphysics.[11] Again, in his encyclical *Fides et Ratio*, Pope John
Paul II challenges in a most salutary way this all too conventional
wisdom of the day: "The word of God refers constantly to things
which transcend human experience and even human thought; but
this 'mystery' could not be revealed, nor could theology render it in
some way intelligible, were human knowledge limited strictly to the
world of sense experience. Metaphysics thus plays an essential role
of mediation in theological research."[12]

As we will see later, for Thomas, in regarding the truth of Eucharistic conversion, it is faith that preserves the human intellect from
deception. This faith, however, does not operate *contra intellectum*,
as an intellectually blind faith, commanded only by divine dictates
to which the will submits in blind obedience—as notoriously conceived in a nominalist Scholastic and postnominalist Protestant theology. Rather this faith is sustained, but not constituted, by the *intellectus fidei*. And the *intellectus fidei* relies on *received* reality—that is,
objective reality. In the case of Eucharistic transubstantiation it is ac-
counted for by a most central *metaphysical* principle, a principle that
antecedes and transcends culture as much as history, human subjec-
tivity as much as the philosophy du jour, in short, the metaphysical
principle of *substance*.[13]

I do not wish to be misunderstood at the very outset. Let me
therefore emphasize unequivocally that metaphysical analysis as
employed by Thomas Aquinas makes possible a profound but not

exhaustive or comprehensive understanding of this central *mystery* of faith—precisely *as* mystery.[14] The subtle metaphysical analysis Thomas employed was not intended to resolve a conceptual or logical problem to everyone's satisfaction and then, after sufficient conceptual clarity had been achieved, to move on to the next problem.[15] For Thomas, Eucharistic transubstantiation is a mystery of faith in the strict sense. Hence, the *intellectus fidei* will explore the mystery by establishing and defending metaphysically its intrinsic, logical possibility. But instead of elevating the mystery from the level of the mere imagination to an allegedly higher plane of a truly conceptual comprehension, along the lines of Hegel's *Begriff* (concept),[16] in its very metaphysical contemplation the *intellectus fidei* will preserve the utterly simple, literal sense of the received dominical words "This is my body which is given for you" (Lk 22:19; RSV), more familiar to Aquinas in its Vulgate rendition, "Hoc est corpus meum quod pro vobis datur."[17]

1

Mysterium Fidei

The Mystery of Faith Proposed
in Sacred Scripture

A contemporary *ressourcement* in the *doctor communis* leads first to a timely and sobering insight: theology proper for Thomas is nothing more and nothing less than holy teaching, *sacra doctrina*. This might strike contemporary sensibilities—informed by principles of historicity, perspectivity, and contextuality—as rather unsophisticated, or worse. For holy teaching, or sacred theology, according to Thomas, is constituted by the simplicity of faith resting on divine authority and embracing the truth as proposed in sacred scripture. After all, it is holy teaching or sacred theology that provides the truths necessary for salvation, as Thomas impresses upon the readers of the *Summa Theologiae* in the very first article of the first question:

It was necessary for man's salvation that there should be a knowledge revealed by God, besides philosophical science built up by human reason. Firstly, indeed, because man is directed to God, as to an end that surpasses the grasp of his reason.... But the end must first be known by men who direct their thoughts and actions to the end. Hence it was necessary for the salvation of man that certain truths which exceed human reason should be made known to him by divine revelation. Even as regards those truths about God which human reason could have discovered, it was necessary that man should be taught by a divine revelation; because the truth about

God such as reason could discover, would only be known by a few, and that after a long time, and with the admixture of many errors. Whereas man's whole salvation, which is in God, depends upon the knowledge of this truth.[18]

True to the understanding of *sacra doctrina* which he put forward in the first question of the *Summa*, when Thomas treats the sacramental conversion in the third part of the *Summa* (q. 75), he dedicates the first article solely to the salvific significance of the real presence as divinely revealed.[19] From this opening article of the question on sacramental conversion it is clear that Thomas understands Christ's real presence in the Eucharist to be a revealed truth conveyed by the literal sense of the inspired scriptures and received by divine faith. It is the revealed mystery of Christ's real presence that motivates Thomas's subsequent metaphysical unfolding or explication of the revealed mystery in q. 75, a. 2. Probing the ontological contours of the revealed mystery with an acute metaphysical analysis is, for Thomas, what it means to give an account of transubstantiation. Truly making explicit the revealed mystery of Christ's real presence in the Eucharist requires developing an account of transubstantiation (see appendix 1, below).

I shall now briefly turn to *ST* III, q. 75, a. 1, first to review Thomas's arguments for the salvific significance of the real presence and, second, to consider the striking way Thomas's arguments manifest the nature of *sacra doctrina*. The three reasons he adduces to affirm "the presence of Christ's true body and blood in this sacrament" are not probative but, rather, are intended to illuminate what is held "by faith alone, which rests upon Divine authority."[20] Each of the reasons Thomas offers draws its strength from a particular perfection that is ordered to salvation: first, in the order of salvation itself, second, in the order of love, and third, in the order of faith.

First, the perfection in the order of salvation. Thomas points out the relationship between the figurative foreshadowing of the sacrifice of Christ's passion in Israel's sacrifices and its fulfillment in Christ's death on the cross, of which the Eucharist is the representation: "Therefore it was necessary that the sacrifice of the New Law instituted by Christ ... should contain Christ Himself crucified, not merely in signification or figure, but also in very truth [*in rei veritate*]. And therefore this sacrament which contains Christ Himself [*quod ipsum Christum realiter continet*], as Dionysius says (*Eccl. Hier.* iii), is perfective of all the other sacraments, in which Christ's virtue is participated."[21]

Second, the perfection in the order of love. It is because of his love for humanity and for the sake of humanity's salvation that "Christ assumed a true body of our nature." Drawing upon a famous insight from Aristotle—an insight that could as well have come from Augustine—that "it is the special feature of friendship to live together with friends," Aquinas refers to Matthew 24:28 in order to point out that Christ promised to his disciples his everlasting bodily presence to them in the world to come. However, as a token of his surpassing friendship and love,

in our pilgrimage He does not deprive us of His bodily presence; but unites us with Himself in this sacrament through the truth of His body and blood. Hence (Jn 6:57) He says: "He that eateth My flesh, and drinketh My blood, abideth in Me, and I in him." Hence this sacrament is the sign of supreme charity, and the uplifter of our hope, from such familiar union of Christ with us.[22]

Third, the perfection in the order of faith. For faith, Thomas argues, pertains to Christ's humanity as much as to his divinity: "And since faith is of things unseen, as Christ shows us His Godhead invisibly, so also in this sacrament He shows us His flesh in an invisible manner."[23]

All three reasons adduced by Thomas illuminate the salvation in service of which *sacra doctrina* stands. This becomes plain when we consider the striking way Thomas displays, in the opening statement of the article, the nature of *sacra doctrina*: "The presence of Christ's true body and blood in this sacrament cannot be detected by sense, nor understanding, but by faith alone [*sola fide*], which rests upon Divine authority. Hence, on Lk 22:19: 'This is My body, which shall be delivered up for you,' Cyril says: 'Doubt not whether this be true; but take rather the Savior's words with faith; for since He is the Truth, He lieth not.'"[24] What Thomas does here is deceptively simple but profoundly significant. First, without quoting it at length (assuming that every reader would know it by heart) he alludes to Christ's words of consecration according to the Gospel of Luke, which are most crucial for the question at hand: "And he took bread, and when he had given thanks he broke it and gave it to them, saying, 'This is my body which is given for you. Do this in remembrance of me.' And likewise the cup after supper, saying, 'This cup which is poured out for you is the new covenant in my blood'" (Lk 22:19–20; RSV). The dominical words themselves, taken in the literal sense, constitute the primordial point of departure for sacred theology, the mode of reception characteristic of positive theology, presupposing that the ultimate author of sacred scripture, the incarnate Word, is speaking directly about himself.

Second, Thomas's argument from the dominical words in Luke 22:19 presuppose that these words are just that: the words of the Lord. But characteristic of positive theology's *modus procedendi*, this presupposition is not simply made axiomatically or aprioristically, to use a modern concept. On the contrary, this very presupposition is itself received, as it represents the church's own understanding of the literal sense. To this purpose, Thomas cites St. Cyril of Alexandria, who—as was already pointed out—enjoins the readers of his own commentary on the Gospel of Luke to take Christ simply at his word because he is the truth: "Doubt not whether this be true; but take rather the Savior's words with faith; for since He is the Truth, He lieth not."[25] That is, Thomas draws the fundamental point about who is speaking about himself in sacred scripture from the words of the one authority among the Greek Fathers who is most intimately associated with the dogma of Chalcedon and who is, next to St. Athanasius, a theologian of quite singular status in the East. Moreover, he prepares this reception of the literal sense in the church's understanding by drawing, in the *sed contra*, upon two Western Fathers,

St. Hilary, bishop of Poitiers, and St. Ambrose, bishop of Milan, both
of whom antedate St. Cyril and hence represent even earlier voices
of the church's undivided tradition, East and West.[26]

An important corollary of Thomas's approach is that the ecclesial mediation of the divine faith that sacred theology entails renders theologically moot the necessity of trying to reconstruct Jesus'
Aramaic diction during the Last Supper—a reconstructive process
whose results are unavoidably provisional not only due to their varying degrees of probability but also to their inherent surpassability
by alternative construals. It would mean to miss a crucial theological point of Thomas's if one were to dismiss his *modus procedendi*
as simply yet another instantiation of the premodern lack of historical awareness. The crucial theological point one would miss with
such a dismissal is that the church's understanding, that is, *traditio* itself, reads this text as *Deus ipse loquitur*. When contemporary
historical-critical exegetes reconstruct the words of consecration as
an early post-Easter tradition instead of attributing them directly to
what they would—according to varying and often mutually exclusive hypotheses—conceive of as the "historical" Jesus, such scholar-
ly results, reflective of a distinctly modern sense of historicity, must
be received into a deeper and theological understanding of the very
apostolic *paradosis* (handing on) whence arose the New Testament.
For this is precisely what *traditio* is all about: the reception of God's
Word in the church that is Christ's body. The post-Easter tradition is
nothing but the hypostatic *paradosis* that announces the truth that
Jesus did indeed take bread and say, "This is my body."

Third, we can observe here what Thomas calls the subalternate
character of the unique science of sacred theology or holy teaching
in the second article of the opening question in the *Summa Theologiae*: "Sacred doctrine [*sacra doctrina*] is a science, because it proceeds
from principles established by the light of a higher science, namely,
the science of God and the blessed [*scientia Dei et beatorum*]. Hence,
just as the musician accepts on authority [*tradita*] the principles
taught him by the mathematician, so sacred science is established

on principles revealed by God [*principia revelata sibi a Deo*]."[27] Returning to q. 75, a. 1, the first move of holy teaching as the uniquely subalternate science is to receive the dominical words of Luke 22:19 by way of the church's understanding (*traditio*) as a truth revealed by God (*principium revelatum a Deo*), that is, a communication of the science of God and the blessed. This truth is not to be interpreted in light of some other more authoritative, profound, or illuminating text of sacred scripture. Rather, in these words, Christ himself has spoken. While God, as the ultimate author of sacred scripture,[28] speaks by way of and through all of them, the dominical words are exceptional as they directly appeal to the immediate assent of faith.

While the primary object of faith is God, the first truth, the assent of faith cannot be immediately to God, but to some propositions, or statements about God. In this life, the primary object of faith, God, the first truth, can only be received by faith through a divine mediation, a definitive revelation—the incarnate Word—as attested in sacred scripture and as rightly interpreted by the church's teaching in form of the articles of faith. In *ST* II-II, q. 5, a. 3, ad 2, he states crisply: "Faith adheres to all the articles of faith by reason of one mean, namely, on account of the First Truth proposed to us in the Scriptures, according to the teaching of the Church who has the right understanding of them."[29] According to the church's right understanding of the first truth, that is, according to the *doctrina Ecclesiae*, in Luke 22:19, "the First Truth proposed to us in the Scriptures" speaks himself and thus constitutes immediately a truth revealed by God (*principium revelatum a Deo*); and St. Cyril's theological judgment (together with St. Hilary's and St. Ambrose's teaching as adduced in the *sed contra*)[30] represents for Thomas paradigmatically "the teaching of the Church that has the right understanding of [the Scriptures]."

Hence, Thomas reminds us in the opening article of the question on the conversion of bread and wine into the body and blood of Christ that *sacra doctrina* is first and foremost the act of faith adhering to the first truth (God) in the concrete instance of its self-communication as apostolically mediated and interpreted by the *doctrina Ecclesiae*.[31] It is upon this doctrinally received and mediated truth revealed by God (*principium revelatum a Deo*) that the *intellectus fidei* draws in its subsequent metaphysical contemplation. Hence, the truth of faith is not established by the profound metaphysical exploration that follows; rather, having been established by the first truth himself and subsequently taught by the *doctrina Ecclesiae*, the truth of faith is illuminated and defended by the discursive probing of the *intellectus fidei*. The truth does not depend on a successful metaphysical defense or even proof; rather, the revealed truth itself elicits the metaphysical contemplation that displays the truth's inherent intelligibility as a mystery of faith and contributes to a more comprehensive and penetrating intellectual reception of it. This is *intellectus fidei*. While the *intellectus fidei* is central to sacred theology, holy teaching (*sacra doctrina*) itself arises from the first truth, the primary author of sacred scripture, and hence, first and foremost, from the incarnate Word himself. There is no other access to this first datum than by way of Christ's body, the church and her teaching.

THE FIRST TRUTH

Wittgenstein rightly observed, "One is unable to notice something—because it is always before one's eyes."[32] Accordingly, it is often the novice or the convert who perceives with fresh eyes what has become all too obvious—and hence invisible—to all those already too accustomed to it, or even tired of it. Erik Peterson was a renowned theologian and historian of dogma. A Lutheran in upbringing and theological training, he was received into the Catholic church on December 25, 1930. Five years earlier, in 1925, in a small but intense treatise on the nature of theology, written in sharp opposition to the rising dialectical theology of Karl Barth, Peterson had pointedly observed:

Just as there has been dogma and the church only since the ascension, so also has there been theology only from this particular point on. One cannot answer the question "what is theology" if one forgets that God's word became flesh and spoke about God. Nor can one answer the question "what is theology" if one forgets the other aspect as well, namely, that Christ ascended to heaven and that there is now dogma.[33]

Dogma, Peterson emphasizes, "does not continue Christ's own discourse about God directly, but rather such that there is now a teaching authority Christ has conferred upon the church in which dogma appears."[34]

I submit that Erik Peterson gleaned this fundamental insight about the nature of theology as *sacra doctrina*—which presupposes revelation, faith, and fidelity—from none other than Thomas Aquinas. In the winter semester of 1923–24, at the Protestant faculty of the University of Göttingen, Peterson had offered a lecture course on Aquinas, an event quite extraordinary in that day and age long before Vatican II, and hence the cause of lively concern in many a quarter of Protestantism.[35] And it is Thomas who states that "the formal object of faith is the First Truth, as manifested in Holy Writ and the teaching of the Church, [which proceeds from the First Truth]."[36] Peterson's rediscovery of theology as *sacra doctrina* is still relevant, possibly even more so in our day when theology has increasingly estranged itself from the formal object of the faith by critical, hermeneutical hyper-sophistication under the rubrics of historical distance, epistemological difference, and cultural plurality. At a time when Protestant liberalism still reigned largely unchecked at most German Protestant university faculties, Peterson learned from Thomas Aquinas that theology as holy teaching (*sacra doctrina*) receives the first truth, God's definitive revelation, proclaimed in sacred scripture as rightly interpreted by the church's magisterium, that is by way of dogma, in the context of the church's comprehensive liturgical and sacramental reality (see appendix 2, below).

Thomas gestures to this mode of receiving the first truth in a hymn he wrote that became part of the new Office of the Blessed Sacrament. He was asked to write this hymn for a new feast that originally arose locally from the church's living faith.[37] On August

11, 1264, in his bull *Transiturus,* Pope Urban IV instituted this feast for the universal church: it is, of course, the feast of Corpus Christi.[38] The sequence for Corpus Christi Mass, *Lauda Sion, Salvatorem,* opens its eleventh stanza with the line "Dogma datur Christianis," which has been translated as "this truth to Christians is proclaimed." In light of the Council of Trent's dogma on Eucharistic conversion and Peterson's profound understanding—according to the mind of Thomas—that the first truth himself speaks about himself in the dominical words of the Gospel, we might render the verse as, "This dogma, this truth from and about the Word himself to Christians is given," namely by way of the *doctrina Ecclesiae,* "that bread passes over [*transit*] into flesh and wine passes over [*transit*] into blood":

> Dogma datur Christianis,
> Quod in carnem transit panis
> Et vinum in sanguinem.
> Quod non capis, quod non vides,
> Animosa firmat fides
> Praeter rerum ordinem.

> This truth to Christians is proclaimed:
> That to flesh, bread is transformed,
> And transformed to blood is wine.
> What you can neither grasp nor see,
> A lively faith will yet affirm
> Beyond this world's design.[39]

2

---:---

Dogma datur Christianis
The Truth Is Given to Christians by
Tradition and the Magisterium

The next step of our *ressourcement* in Thomas's procedure of holy teaching (*sacra doctrina*) is to consider "the teaching of the Church who has the right understanding of [the Scriptures]" (*doctrina Ecclesiae*). As the Second Vatican Council did not produce any new dogmatic definitions, and as the dogmatic definitions of the First Vatican Council have no immediate bearing upon our topic, the most recent relevant council is the Council of Trent. The more proximate normative context, however, is constituted by the teaching of the ordinary magisterium in its ongoing affirmation of the decree of Trent. To put it negatively, for theology, properly understood as sacred theology or holy teaching (*sacra doctrina*), the proximate normative context can never be the critically established hermeneutical pre-understanding (*Vorverständnis*) of contemporary thought (the predominant intellectual climate, in German called *Zeitgeist*), nor the findings of the sciences, nor the variant cultural contexts of the faithful. All of these concerns have their proper place in subsequent kerygmatic, catechetical, and apologetic tasks of communicating, teaching, and defending the faith. But theology, properly understood as holy teaching (*sacra doctrina*), first *actively receives* the church's understanding—"this truth to Christians is proclaimed" (*dogma datur Christianis*), as Thomas felicitously expressed it in his hymn—by way of the magisterial teaching of the twentieth and early twenty-first centuries.

For our task of inquiring into the mystery of the Eucharist, four encyclicals are pertinent: Pope Leo XIII's *Mirae Caritatis* (1902), Pope Pius XII's *Mediator Dei* (1947), Pope Paul VI's *Mysterium Fidei* (1965), and Pope John Paul II's *Ecclesia de Eucharistia* (2003). The first two encyclicals treat the Eucharist in a comprehensive way and especially focus on the Eucharistic sacrifice. I will cite them only very briefly, for it is only with Pope Paul VI, in the immediate aftermath of the Second Vatican Council and in light of new theological interpretations (emerging especially in the Netherlands) of the mystery of Christ's real presence, that an explicit magisterial averment of Eucharistic transubstantiation became necessary. Pope John Paul II, in *Ecclesia de Eucharistia*, as well as in the recent universal *Catechism of the Catholic Church* (1994; editio typica 1997), reaffirms Paul VI's emphasis in the encyclical *Mysterium Fidei*, which is arguably the most important magisterial intervention in the twentieth century on the specific topic of Eucharistic transubstantiation.

In both *Mirae Caritatis* and *Mediator Dei*, the primary emphasis lies on the inherent link between Christ's self-offering on the cross and the Eucharistic sacrifice. Pope Leo XIII, in *Mirae Caritatis*, teaches that

the Eucharist, according to the testimony of the holy Fathers, should be regarded as in a manner a continuation and extension of the Incarnation. For in and by it the substance of the incarnate Word is united with individual men, and the supreme Sacrifice offered on Calvary is in a wondrous manner renewed.... And this miracle, itself the very greatest of its kind, is accompanied by innumerable other miracles; for here all the laws of nature are suspended; the whole substance of the bread and wine are changed into the Body and the Blood; the species of bread and wine are sustained by the divine power without the support of any underlying substance; the Body of Christ is present in many places at the same time, that is to say, wherever the Sacrament is consecrated. (par. 7)

In his extensive and rich encyclical *Mediator Dei*, Pope Pius XII re-affirms the teaching of Trent:

The august sacrifice of the altar ... is no mere empty commemoration of the passion and death of Jesus Christ, but a true and proper act of sacrifice, whereby the High Priest by an unbloody immolation offers Himself as a most acceptable victim to the Eternal Father, as He did upon the cross. (par. 68)

Likewise the victim is the same, namely, our divine Redeemer in His human nature with His true body and blood. The manner, however, in which Christ is offered is different.... For by the "transubstantiation" of bread into the body of Christ and of wine into His blood, His body and blood are both really present: now the eucharistic species under which He is present symbolize the actual separation of His body and blood. Thus the commemorative representation of His death, which actually took place on Calvary, is repeated in every sacrifice of the altar, seeing that Jesus Christ is symbolically shown by separate symbols to be in a state of victimhood. (par. 70)

Christ's real presence in the Eucharistic sacrifice is affirmed precisely in the way the Council of Trent defined the matter. However, Eucharistic transubstantiation, while unequivocally affirmed, remains in the background of both encyclicals. This changes drastically with Pope Paul VI's encyclical *Mysterium Fidei*, when it comes to the forefront. Why?

During the Second Vatican Council, the Dogmatic Constitution *Lumen Gentium*, no. 11, had clearly, if tersely, affirmed the teaching of Eucharistic sacrifice as laid down extensively in Pope Pius XII's *Mediator Dei*. Arguably, because of various new and not altogether unproblematic attempts at a new interpretation of the mystery of Christ's real presence in the Eucharist, *Mysterium Fidei* has the function of an explicit magisterial *addendum* on a most central aspect of Eucharistic doctrine, which was left unaddressed by Vatican II. Indeed, the opening paragraphs of *Mysterium Fidei* make it quite clear that this magisterial intervention is to be understood along these lines. Because *Mysterium Fidei* is affirmed by *Ecclesia de Eucharistia* and by the *Catechism of the Catholic Church*, it is advisable to attend more closely to this particular encyclical.

In *Mysterium Fidei*, Pope Paul VI addresses most directly the "dogma of transubstantiation" (par. 10) and declares unequivocally that it is impermissible

> to discuss the mystery of transubstantiation without mentioning what the Council of Trent had to say about the marvelous conversion of the whole substance of the bread into the Body and the whole substance of the wine into the Blood of Christ, as if they involve nothing more than "transignification," or "transfinalization" as they call it; or ... to propose and act upon the opinion that Christ Our Lord is no longer present in the consecrated Hosts that remain after the celebration of the sacrifice of the Mass has been completed. (par. 11)

After having, by way of the words of St. Bonaventure, unequivocally affirmed Christ's real presence in the sacrament as indispensable for the integrity of the true Catholic faith, Pope Paul VI turns to what some contemporary theologians might call proper "word care": "Once the integrity of the faith has been safeguarded, then it is time to guard the proper way of expressing it, lest our careless use of words give rise, God forbid, to false opinions regarding faith in the most sublime things" (par. 23). In order to appreciate what such theological "word care" entails for Paul VI, we must turn to some longer passages from pars. 24–25. Here Paul VI describes in quite exact terms the way sacred theology is to receive the Church's understanding by way of the definitions of dogma, and the precise nature of the very concepts that the definitions of dogma employ:

> And so *the rule of language which the Church has established through the long labor of centuries, with the help of the Holy Spirit, and which she has confirmed with the authority of the Councils, and which has more than once been the watchword and banner of orthodox faith, is to be religiously preserved, and no one may presume to change it at his own pleasure or under the pretext of new knowledge.* Who would ever tolerate that the dogmatic formulas used by the ecumenical councils for the mysteries of the Holy Trinity and the Incarnation be judged as no longer appropriate for men of our times and let others be rashly substituted for them? In the same way, *it cannot be tolerated that any individual should, on his own authority, take something away from the formulas which were used by the Council of Trent to propose the Eucharis-*

tic Mystery for our belief. These formulas—like the others that the Church used to propose the dogmas of faith—express concepts that are not tied to a certain specific form of human culture, or to a certain level of scientific progress, or to one or another theological school. Instead they *set forth what the human mind grasps of reality through necessary and universal experience and what it expresses in apt and exact words, whether it be in ordinary or more refined language. For this reason, these formulas are adapted to all men of all times and all places.* (par. 24; emphasis added)

They can, it is true, be made clearer and more obvious; and doing this is of great benefit. But it must always be done in such a way that they retain the meaning in which they have been used, so that with the advance of an understanding of the faith, the truth of faith will remain unchanged. For it is the teaching of the First Vatican Council that "the meaning that Holy Mother the Church has once declared, is to be retained forever, and no pretext of deeper understanding ever justifies any deviation from that meaning."[40] (par. 25)

After delineating these dogmatic guidelines for the ongoing work of sacred theology, *Mysterium Fidei* applies them directly to Christ's real presence in the Eucharist:

This presence is called "real" not to exclude the idea that the others are "real" too, but rather to indicate presence *par excellence*, because it is substantial and through it Christ becomes present whole and entire, God and man.[41] And so it would be wrong for anyone to try to explain this manner of presence by dreaming up a so-called "pneumatic" nature of the glorious body of Christ that would be present everywhere; or for anyone to limit it to symbolism, as if this most sacred Sacrament were to consist in nothing more than an efficacious sign "of the spiritual presence of Christ and of His intimate union with the faithful, the members of His Mystical Body."[42] (par. 39)

Three aspects of *Mysterium Fidei* are immediately pertinent to our topic of consideration. First, theological proposals of transignification and transfinalization do not constitute sufficient interpretations of the Council of Trent's teaching of the sacramental conversion of the whole substance of bread into the body of Christ and the whole substance of wine into the blood of Christ. While possibly adding helpful aspects, these proposals cannot replace an ontological account of transubstantiation. Second, according to the Council of Trent, the real presence of Christ in the Eucharist signifies a *substantial* presence. The encyclical's emphasis on Christ substantial presence opposes alternative accounts that would interpret Christ's real presence in the Eucharist by way of a doctrine of the ubiquity of Christ's glorious body everywhere in the universe (a position argued by Lutheran theologians) or by way of a doctrine of Christ's dynamic presence by way of the sacramental signs (a position argued by Calvinist theologians). Third, *Mysterium Fidei* is clear that over the course of a long period of time, the church has established—with the aid of the Holy Spirit—a rule of dogmatic and doctrinal language that is actually adapted to all people at all times. The Council of Trent's teaching on sacramental conversion is one instance of this rule. Hence, the received language may not be changed or replaced by other words and concepts advanced by individual theologians. Rather, the substantial presence of Christ in the Eucharist must be maintained, both in words and also in the clearest possible explication of these words—which will have to be an ontological explication of the conversion of one whole substance into another whole substance.

Turning now to Pope John Paul II's encyclical *Ecclesia de Eucharistia*, we can be very brief. For regarding Christ's real presence in the Eucharist and sacramental conversion, the encyclical cites *Mysterium Fidei* directly and explicitly reaffirms the teaching of the Council of Trent:

The sacramental re-presentation of Christ's sacrifice, crowned by the resurrection, in the Mass involves a most special presence which—in the words of Paul VI—"*is called 'real' not as a way of excluding all other types of presence as if they were 'not real,' but because it is a presence in the fullest sense: a substantial presence whereby Christ, the God-Man, is wholly and entirely present.*" This sets forth once more the perennially valid teaching of the Council of Trent: "the consecration of the bread and wine effects the change of the whole substance of the bread into the substance of the body of Christ our Lord, and of the whole substance of the wine into the substance of his blood. And the holy Catholic Church has fittingly and properly called this change transubstantiation." Truly the Eucharist is a *mysterium fidei*, a mystery which surpasses our understanding and can only be received in faith, as is often brought out in the catechesis of the Church Fathers regarding this divine sacrament: "Do not see"—Saint Cyril of Jerusalem exhorts—"in the bread and wine merely natural elements, because the Lord has expressly said that they are his body and his blood: faith assures you of this, though your senses suggest otherwise."[43] (par. 15; emphasis added)

Finally, also drawing upon Pope Paul VI's encyclical *Mysterium Fidei*, the *Catechism of the Catholic Church* unequivocally reaffirms, in one accord with the above encyclicals, the teaching of the Council of Trent that Christ is substantially present in the sacrament and that this substantial presence comes about through a change of the whole substance of the bread and wine into the substance of the body and blood of Christ.[44]

Let us step back now and gather some of the findings of the magisterium's teaching as they orient *sacra doctrina* in its active reception of the truth as proposed in sacred scripture. Several observations are in order. The magisterium's teaching in the twentieth and the early twenty-first centuries (most explicitly in the encyclical *Mysterium Fidei*) makes it very hard, if not impossible, to deny that (1) the Council of Trent's teaching on Eucharistic sacrifice and Eucharistic transubstantiation continues to hold and that (2) the magisterium maintains a normative hermeneutic for understanding these dogmatic definitions. These dogmatic definitions are made up of true propositions with respect to their object (*quoad rem*), the object (*res*) here referring to principles that transcend historical change and cultural context. It is, furthermore, hard, if not impossible, to deny that (3) the magisterium indeed assumes that the basic prephilosophical apprehension of reality already entails certain metaphysical principles pertaining to being and essence on which from early on the dogmatic tradition has drawn. These presuppositions were not invented by classical metaphysics but, rather, systematically clarified and analyzed with a lasting, fruitful pertinence. In addition, it is hard, if not impossible, to deny that (4) the magisterium maintains that the decree of Trent contains in and of itself theological accounts that specify certain truths of faith proposed in sacred scripture—theological accounts that are not again and again in need of further theological accounts that reinterpret the accounts that were given by the council Fathers at Trent. For these theological accounts entailed in the decree of Trent rely not on explanations that are historically relative, but on metaphysical principles that arise from reality itself. Finally, it seems hard, if not impossible, to deny that (5) the magisterium assumes that these dogmatic propositions, as theological statements, intend God *as well as* the essence of things and hence presuppose certain abiding metaphysical principles. Hence, it seems quite obvious that while the magisterium does not endorse the teaching of any one particular theological school, it is concerned to avoid the danger and problem of the late-medieval "double accounting," as then Joseph Ratzinger once aptly called it.[45] Such "double accounting" means that while faith and dogma might say one thing—say, "transubstantiation"—philosophy, accountable to natural reason alone, will inevitably think quite another thing— say, "consubstantiation" or "transfinalization" or something else.

In our particular case, the magisterium teaches unequivocally that the decree of Trent clearly presupposes a prephilosophical common knowledge of substance and hence draws on the abiding metaphysical principle of substance.[46] Furthermore, the magisterium has unequivocally rejected the notion that "transubstantiation" might serve as a mere signifier in a quasi-nominalist sense, that is, as a notional placeholder for a range of interpretations that might only in the widest of senses fall under it. Hence, it seems extremely hard, if not simply impossible, for Catholic dogmatic theology, conceived as *sacra doctrina*, to give support to the widely held opinion that the dogmatic formulations decreed by the Council of Trent regarding Eucharistic conversion contain a doctrinal "intention" that can, and indeed must, be isolated from its conceptual "explanation," an explanation that expresses an essentially ineffable truth with respect to us (*quoad nos*), whereby the explanation remains inherently contingent upon the historical situation from which it arises. A rejection of such a specious hermeneutics of dogma, however, does not foreclose the possibility of some analogous hermeneutical approximation of what the dogma intends in contexts in which it is hard to communicate the depth of the principles presupposed by the dogma.[47]

3

Eucharistic Conversion and the Categories "Substance" and "Quantity"

Given the clearly defined magisterial teaching on transubstantiation, contemporary dogmatic theology requires a fresh *ressourcement* of Thomas's positive and speculative theology. Thomas's profound and compelling doctrine of Christ's Eucharistic presence offers itself anew because it grants surpassing intelligibility to the principles entailed in the doctrine of transubstantiation and especially to the abiding *metaphysical* notion of substance. This claim might come as a surprise to many, for Edward Schillebeeckx, OP, in a small but influential work on the Eucharist, without offering any reasons or evidence, expresses a widespread opinion when he makes the sweeping claim that "the facts of modern physics had shaken neo-scholastic speculations about the concept of substance to their foundations.... The quantum theory in physics made many neo-scholastics realize that the concept *substance* could not be applied to material reality—or at the most that the whole of the cosmos could be seen as only one great substance."[48]

Numerous modern scientists, first and foremost among them Michael Polanyi, Ian G. Barbour, and Arthur C. Peacocke, would sharply disagree with the tacit implication of Schillebeeckx's judgment that quantum mechanics would call for the kind of atomistic

analytic philosophy that would render the talk about substance vac-
uous.[49] Jacques Maritain offers an account of the fundamental difference between the metaphysical concept of substance and the matter
and energy of the natural scientist that is still as salient today as it
was when he first committed it to paper. Because of its importance
the passage is worth being cited in full:

> When the physicist speaks of matter (or mass) and energy and declares
> that matter can be transformed into energy and vice versa, he is in no way
> thinking of what the philosopher calls the substance of material things—
> this substance, considered in itself (abstracted from its accidents) is
> purely intelligible and cannot be known by sense or any means of ob-
> servation and measurement. The matter and energy of the physicist are
> physico-mathematical entities elaborated by the mind in view of express-
> ing the reality; this corresponds symbolically to that which the philoso-
> pher calls the *proper accidents* or the structural properties of the material
> substance (quantity and quality). What we can say then, *from the philos-
> opher's point of view or from ontological knowledge* is, that the material sub-
> stance considered in one or the other of the elements of the periodic table
> (which is revealed to us in a merely symbolic manner, under the aspect
> of the atom of the physicist) possesses in virtue of its proper accidents or
> structural properties a certain *organization in space* (which is revealed to us
> in a symbolic manner under the characteristics of the system of electrons,
> protons, neutrons etc. of the physicist) and a *specific activity* which derives
> from its very essence (and which is revealed to us in a symbolic manner
> as "energy" invested in the system in question). Then, when it is a case
> of atomic transmutations, the change which is produced in the system of
> electrons—for example, the loss of an electron due to some atomic bom-
> bardment—will be regarded by the philosopher as a *symbolic image* (in the
> field of physico-mathematical entities) of what constitutes ontologically
> the ultimate disposition of the matter, which determines the substantial
> change the instant that the previous substance is "corrupted" and the new
> substance is "generated."[50]

Maritain helps us understand why it is a fallacious inference to
draw from the demise of Aristotle's philosophy of nature among the
natural scientists of the seventeenth and eighteenth century and
from the rise of quantum mechanics in the twentieth century the
conclusion that the metaphysical concept of substance has become

utterly passé. Quite to the contrary, it is, I submit, the metaphysical concept of substance—as deployed in Thomas's metaphysical elucidation of the Eucharistic mystery—that saves the Tridentine dogmatic notion of complete substantial conversion from turning into a doctrinally protected, but nevertheless mere metaphor. Let us recall that the Council of Trent solemnly decreed that: "By the consecration of the bread and wine, there takes place the change [*conversio*] of the whole substance of the bread into the substance of the body of Christ our Lord, and of the whole substance of the wine into the substance of his blood. And the holy catholic church has suitably and properly called this change transubstantiation" (see appendix 3, below).[51]

The encyclical *Fides et Ratio* reminds us by way of Thomas Aquinas that sacred theology receives divine truth "proposed to us in the Sacred Scriptures and rightly interpreted by the Church's teaching."[52] Hence, sacred theology continues to be faced with the task of the *intellectus fidei*, that is, the task of understanding what conversion of a whole substance into another substance entails. It is in this way that sacred theology continues to be faced with the ongoing reception of Thomas's profound and profoundly satisfying metaphysical interpretation of the mystery of Eucharistic conversion.

SUBSTANCE

What is "substance" as Thomas receives the notion from Aristotle's philosophical analysis of reality and as he deploys it theologically? Before we address this question, it is imperative to recall that Thomas understands philosophy to be an ordered set of inquiries. Referring to Thomas's commentary on the neo-Platonic *Liber de causis*, Ralph McInerny identifies three "disarming assumptions" that capture Thomas's understanding of philosophy in a nutshell. They are "1) that all philosophers are in principle engaged in the same enterprise; 2) that truths he has learned from Aristotle are simply truths, not 'Aristotelian tenets'; and 3) consequently that such truths as one finds in Neoplatonism or anywhere else must be compatible with truths already known. This is the basis for saying that Thomism is not a *kind* of philosophy."[53]

Hence, it would be profoundly wrong, although not at all un-common, to assume that Thomas submits a "theory" of the Eucha-ristic conversion. Rather, always proceeding conceptually from what is easier to what is more difficult to understand, he analogically ex-tends the "natural hearing," the inquiry into material being and sub-sequently into immaterial being as undertaken in Aristotle's *Physics* and extended in his *Metaphysics*, in order to guide the metaphysical contemplation into what remains irreducibly a mystery of faith. The *intellectus*, however, inevitably takes its departure, by analogical ex-tension, from the world we know.[54] And at the center of the world we know is "substance," because, as the noted metaphysician Law-rence Dewan observes, "all things that are, depend for their existence on substances."[55] For this very reason, "substance, along with 'a be-ing,' belongs to the domain of what all naturally know. Metaphysi-cal reflection can only serve to render that knowledge less subject to impediments."[56]

Consequently, in the present intellectual context one can nev-er recall often enough that—as the distinguished Thomist philoso-pher John Wippel aptly put it—Thomas holds first and foremost in his theory of knowledge that "the order of thought is based upon the order of reality and reflects it. Because words in turn reflect thoughts, by attending to distinctive modes of predication we may ultimately discern different modes of being."[57] Differently put, "supreme and di-verse modes of predication (as expressed in the predicaments) ... fol-low from and depend upon supreme and diverse modes of being."[58] Hence, according to Thomas, we discover these supreme modes of being precisely by attending to the diverse modes of predication.[59]

The classical locus for Thomas's exposition of this fundamental insight of Aristotle is his commentary on Aristotle's *Physics* III:

[Being] is divided according to the diverse modes of existing. But modes of existing are proportional to the modes of predicating. For when we predicate something of another, we say this is that. Hence the ten genera of being are called the ten predicaments. Now every predication is made in one of three ways. One way is when that which pertains to the essence is predicated of some subject, as when I say Socrates is a man, or man is animal. The predicament of substance is taken in this way.[60]

A predicament denotes the character, status, or classification assigned by a predication. This character, status, or classification is a category. Aristotle's list of categories (substance or being and nine accidents: quantity, quality, relation, place, time, posture, having or possession, action, and passion) comprise a possibly exhaustive set of classes among which all things might be distributed. Let us take the example of a rabbit: substance (the rabbit); quantity (has four legs); quality (is furry and brown); relation (is larger than a mouse and smaller than a dog or a horse); place (is in the room); time (we bought it a week ago); posture (sits upright on its four legs); having or possession (has four legs); action (eats a carrot); passion (is patted by me). Aristotle thus marks off substances (such as a rabbit or a tree or a human being) from all other categories of beings. He distinguishes between *primary substances* (individuals; things that cannot be predicated of anything or to be said to be in anything) and *secondary substances* (the species and genera of the primary substances, differently put, the kinds under which the primary substances are found). Peter is a primary substance, while human being is a secondary substance. Human being is predicated of Peter, and hence all that is predicated of human being is predicated of Peter.[61] In the following, substance will be considered exclusively in the sense of primary substance.

A primary substance signifies what subsists in itself (*ens in se*) in differentiation from accidents that exist only in another (*ens in alio*), that is, in a primary substance. Thomas calls the primary substance "the subsistent thing" (*ens per se*), yet he does not take self-subsistent being to be a proper definition of substance.[62] "Substance is not rightly defined as a self-subsistent being."[63] In a marked departure from Aristotle, Thomas rather understands "what exists in itself" (*ens per se*) as merely an accurate description of the subsistence that is proper to substance; for the existence (*esse*) of a substance is not from itself (*ex se*) but rather is received; its act of being (*actus essendi*) is a participation in the gift of created being itself (*ipsum esse creatum*), the closest created similitude of the uncreated divine essence.[64] This subtle but significant difference between Aristotle and Thomas on the understanding of substance marks the crucial difference between Aristotle's first philosophy, which is a metaphysics of substance, and Thomas's philosophy of being, which is a metaphysics of creation. According to Thomas, the subsistence of substance is not absolute, but contingent; only creatures can be substances. God is not a substance, because God's essence (*essentia*) is not distinct from God's being (*esse*). As the subsistent act of existence itself (*ipsum esse subsistens*) God is above all substance. Like God, created substances indeed subsist in their being. But unlike God, created substances not only receive their being (*esse*), but also a distinct limitation of their being by way of their essence (*essentia*).[65] Every substance has a twofold ontological signature, so to speak: (1) the reception of existence (*esse*) by way of participation through the act of being (*actus essendi*) in created being itself (*ipsum esse creatum*) and (2) the reception of each substance's distinct "whatness" (*quidditas*) by way of a principle or cause (*essentia*) that limits being (*esse*).

Substance, essence, and nature express the same reality. But *essence*—in distinction from substance—signifies that by virtue of which something is what it is. *Nature* signifies the substance as a subsistent and unified principle of activity. Created substances come as separate substances (angels; and in a certain way also the spiritual soul) and as material substances. Every material substance has need of further perfections, called accidents, which are connoted by the remaining nine categories of Aristotle's list. Quantity and quality differ from the other accidents in that they are *per se* or proper accidents of material substances, quantity in an absolute way, and quality in a derived way, mediated by quantity. Substance and proper or *per se* accidents stand in mutual relation, as a proper or *per se* accident is a principle that complements material substance and together with it, through their common existence, constitutes the individually existing thing. It is the substance that properly "has being" and therefore is "a being" (*ens per se*); an accident, by contrast, is more properly "of a being."[66]

ARE BREAD AND WINE SUBSTANCES?

By distinguishing substance from its accidents, Thomas is laying the ground to distinguish the substance of the Eucharist from the accidents of bread and wine that remain. However, Thomas is faced with an objection. Are bread and wine substances at all? Thomas holds the view that no artifacts are substances.[67] Rather, natural beings and especially living beings are substances. Thomas's understanding of what does and what does not qualify as a substance raises, of course, the question whether the preconsecratory Eucharistic elements, bread and wine, are indeed substances or whether they might rather be artifacts. Thomas puts this question to himself as an objection to his thesis that the substantial form of the bread (which is a constituting principle of substance) does not remain after the consecration: "It seems that the substantial form of the bread remains in this sacrament after the consecration. For it has been said [*ST* III, q. 75, a. 5] that the accidents remain after the consecration. But since bread is an artificial thing [*quiddam artificiale*], its form is an accident. Therefore, it remains after the consecration."[68] The response that Thomas offers to this objection appears, especially to the hurried contemporary reader, puzzling—to say the least:

There is nothing to prevent art [*ars*] from making a thing whose form is not an accident, but a substantial form; as frogs and serpents can be produced by art: for art produces such forms not by its own power, but by the power of natural energies [*virtute naturalium principiorum*]. And in this way, it produces the substantial forms of bread, by the power of fire baking the matter made up of flour and water.[69]

Some interpreters take Thomas to appeal in his response to the established opinion held from Aristotle up to Kant that the pro-

cess of putrefaction, the rotting of organic material, could gener-
ate worms, flies, maggots, etc.[70] This purported process of generation was called "equivocal generation" (*generatio aequivoca*) because
it was understood to be essentially different from regular natural
generation. With the rise of modern natural sciences, the theory of
equivocal generation was, of course, quickly discarded. Does Thomas's response therefore depend on a piece of outdated natural philosophy? Does he make his ontological interpretation of the Eucharistic mystery rely on a passé philosophy of nature?

A first indication that this interpretation might be flawed is the
fact that in his response Thomas does not use "putrefaction" (*putre-
factio*)—a term to be found 132 times in the *Corpus thomisticum*. Furthermore, the usual outcome of equivocal generation was understood to be maggots, fruit flies, etc., not frogs and serpents. In light
of these indications one might be well advised to discard equivocal
generation as the implied referent in Thomas's response and to recall instead that Thomas is a theologian and commentator of the sacred page (*sacra pagina*). His reference to frogs and serpents sends
the mind of bible-literate Dominican student brothers (as it should
everyone else) not to equivocal generation but to Egypt and to the
Book of Exodus's account of Moses's confrontation with Pharaoh
and his magicians right before the flight of the Israelites from Egypt.
According to Exodus 7:12, "Every [magician] cast down his rod, and
it became a serpent" (RSV). And according to Exodus 8:7, "The magicians did the same by their secret arts and brought frogs upon the
land of Egypt" (RSV). Thomas is referring—obliquely for modern
scripturally illiterate readers but obviously for his Dominican students—to a narrative account in sacred scripture where human art
(*ars*), albeit secret (as the occult arts are), with the help of the power of natural energies (*virtute naturalium principiorum*), produces
natural beings, hence, substances. In virtue of their distinct kind of
coming about—human art (*ars*)—they are artificial objects; but in
virtue of their proper nature, they are natural beings and hence substances rather than artifacts.

In a lucid essay, Christopher M. Brown unpacks Thomas's line of reasoning: "Some substances can be aided in their generation by human art. But an artisan's aiding the generation of a natural thing is not a sufficient condition for that natural thing's being considered an artifact."[71] Thomas takes the literal sense of the narrative accounts of Exodus 7 and 8 at face value. He thus has access to a case where magicians by secret human art with the help of the power of natural energies produce natural beings, substances. Thomas argues that a baker, by analogy, produces bread by way of human art with the help of the power of natural energies. The secret art of the magicians does not produce the substantial forms of the frogs and serpents by its own power but rather by the power of the natural energies. Similarly, the baker's art does not produce the substantial form of the bread by its own power but rather by the power of the natural energies. In neither case does the intervention of human art create a sufficient condition for the natural thing's being to be considered an artifact. In the case of obvious artifacts, like hammers, knives, violins, and houses, human art imposes a form that is completely extrinsic to the natural things from which the artifact is made. It is an accidental form, the exclusive result of the intervention of human art.

For modern readers, the Exodus account of the magicians' secret art obviously entails too many interpretive and hermeneutical problems to serve as a compelling analogy for Thomas's understanding of bread's being as that of a natural thing that *qua* natural thing has a substantial and not merely accidental form. The modern reader might, however, be able to accept the process of cloning as an appropriate if not compelling contemporary analogy. By the human art of biotechnology and with the help of the power of natural energies, scientists can produce frogs, snakes, and even mammals. It is not the bioengineer's art that produces the cloned animals by its own power but rather by the power of the natural energies, the genetically guided biochemical processes on the molecular, cellular, and macro-organic levels. The cloned animals, because of the way they come about, are artificial objects, yet because they are obviously living beings, they have all the constitutive characteristics of natural things that have substantial forms. Also, quite obviously, the kind of animals produced by cloning, come about usually in the way living things reproduce, that is, by processes of natural generation. In the case of cloning, the intervention of human art obviously does not create a sufficient condition for the natural thing's being to be considered an artifact. The natural processes to which a highly sophisticated kind of human intervention is conducive produces the substantial form of a living being.

Now, what would be a sufficient reason for a natural thing's being to be considered an artifact? What makes artificial objects and artifacts similar is, quite obviously, the intervention of human art. Hence, the sufficient reason we are looking for would have to arise from the role the intervention of human art plays in the constitution of the thing (*res*). Artificial objects like the ones presently under consideration (bread and wine; cloned frogs and snakes) are not the kind of things that would absolutely require the intervention of human art as one of their necessary efficient causes (as would, for example, hammers, knives, violins, and houses). The coming about of a hammer, a knife, a violin, or a house requires absolutely the intervention of human art as one of its efficient causes (next to the power of natural energies). If a hammer, a knife, or a violin exists, we must posit that one of the efficient causes bringing about these objects was human art. This is not necessarily the case with bread and wine; under certain favorable conditions, they may come about naturally. While this is quite obvious in the case of wine, one might legitimately wonder whether flour and some water could become bread without the intervention of human art. Even if flour and water could on their own come together somehow without such an intervention, humans make flour. While it is true that usually humans make flour, it is necessary to remember that flour is nothing but the result of grains being crushed. This can, even if very rarely, occur by way of natural processes without the intervention of human art. Water and heat are natural things and crushed grains may come about by natural processes. Undoubtedly, the intervention of human art is conducive in bringing them together in such a way that in each case bread is the result of their coming together. But the intervention of human art is not *essential* in this case as it is in the coming about of a hammer, a knife, a violin, or a house. Hence, what creates a sufficient reason to consider a thing an artifact—even if all its component parts are again natural things—is this: the intervention of human art has to be essential and not merely conducive to the coming about of the thing. This is the reason why being brought about by the human art of the baker with the help of the power of natural energies does not create a sufficient reason to consider the outcome an artifact. And what is not an artifact, has a substantial form and therefore is a substance. As Brown correctly observes: "This is because the processes that are essential to generating the bread in the first place are natural ones, for example, the heating of a mixture of flour and water by fire."[72] Human intervention is merely conducive for generating of bread and wine. Brown rightly concludes: "Therefore, since being baked by art is not essential to bread—and like some wine or a frog this piece of bread belongs to a kind that can occur naturally—it is reasonable to think with Aquinas that this piece of bread is a *substance* fit for transubstantiation."[73] This, in a nutshell, is Thomas's own argument (admittedly quite abbreviated and condensed) that bread and wine have substantial forms and, consequently, that these forms do not remain after the consecration.[74]

QUANTITY

If we were to consider substance in general, the above would suffice. But in Eucharistic conversion we deal with the conversion of *material* substances. And material substances, as just stated, stand in need of further perfections besides the act of being (*actus essendi*). Because of this, we need to consider briefly the one accident that is necessarily proper to material substance and that is, therefore, in a certain sense, an absolute *per se* accident for material substance: *quantity*. Let us first return to Thomas's fifth lecture on Aristotle's *Physics* III: "Another mode is that in which that which is not of the essence of a thing, but which inheres in it, is predicated of a thing. This is found either on the part of the matter of the subject, and thus is the predicament of quantity (for quantity properly follows upon matter …), or else it follows upon the form, and thus is the predicament of quality."[75]

Significantly, in Thomas's listing of the categories (or predicaments), quantity is listed right after substance, here implicitly understood as a sensible, material thing. For example, in the process of generation, matter antecedes form, as matter is what form reduces to a particular substance. Hence quantity antecedes quality. For while quantity inheres immediately in the material substance, quality inheres mediately in the material substance by inhering in quantity. For this very reason, quantity is the first accident of the substance of a sensible, material thing.[76] Interestingly, however, quantity itself cannot be properly defined, as it has no *genus proximum*. Thomas and the Thomist tradition, therefore, tended to circumscribe it by saying that it entails parts and divisibility into integral, quantitative parts.[77]

Quantity is a determination of being which gives extension to a material substance; hence it is called "dimensive" quantity. Without quantity, a material substance would have no distinguishable parts, no parts outside of parts (*partes extra partes*). Everything would, as Leo Elders puts it, "flow into each other" in the sense that there would be no spatial relationship anymore between the parts.[78] While quantity gives to material substance its dimensions, its intrinsic measure by way of the order of parts, the parts themselves are constituted and sustained by the substance itself.[79] The latter circumstance reminds us that, indeed, quantity modifies the being of substance by giving it the extension of space and hence relates *intrinsically* to the substance. For this reason, quantity may be called the "first" or "absolute" accident of a material substance. Quantity, the first accident of a material substance, inheres in the substance itself while the other accidents modify the being of substance by way of the first inhering accident, dimensive quantity.[80]

However, in contrast with other Scholastic theologians, Thomas and the later Thomist tradition insist on the real distinction between

substance and quantity. While quantity always gives spatial extension to something that subsists in itself, there is no identity between
substance and quantity. The latter is a real accident and, indeed, the
first accident of material substances. Every substance composed of
matter and form requires the first or immediately inherent accident
of quantity. For in order to be itself, that is, *this* material substance,
it requires dimensive quantity, the specific order of parts outside of
parts. Dimensive quantity, in short, contributes to individuation. As
philosopher Joseph Bobik puts it:

> Dimensive quantity is quantity having within itself *partes extra partes*. It
> has within itself *distinguishable* parts outside other *distinguishable* parts....
> And the scholastic formula in turn brings out the unique vitality of dimen-
> sive quantity as a principle capable of contributing to individuation. By
> their very spread-out-ness or extendedness, the parts of dimensive quan-
> tity are situated or posited outside (*extra*) each other. Because of their
> very spread-out-ness, these parts cannot enter into each other so that they
> would coincide. By their very extendedness, these parts exclude each oth-
> er, and are hence distinguishable from each other. By their very spread-
> out-ness within the whole, each requires a diverse situation or position in
> relation to the others within the whole.[81]

We can begin to anticipate the central role the categories substance
and quantity play in Thomas's metaphysical elucidation of the theological truth that indeed nothing less than the whole Christ is contained under this sacrament.

REAL CONCOMITANCE—PERSONAL PRESENCE

One might ask whether Thomas's concentration on the categories
of substance and quantity in the elucidation of the Eucharistic mystery is ever so subtly reductive, in that such a concentration ultimately distracts from the fact that Christ's sacramental presence is
a fundamentally personal presence? Might not the focus on "substance" and "quantity" give rise to a Eucharistic "essentialism" that
obscures the fact that Christ's presence is irreducibly personal?

In order to address this question, we must realize first of all that the terminus of the Eucharistic conversion is the substance of Christ's body in its respective present state. At the Last Supper, Christ was present to the twelve apostles in his natural mode as the incarnate Son of the Father instituting the Eucharist and thereby marking the very beginning of "his hour," his self-oblation to the Father on the cross for the sake of "the many." His sacramental, substantial presence in the sacrament at the Last Supper was that of his earthly bodily existence in its concrete state at the beginning of his passion. Theologian Charles Journet puts the matter succinctly: "At the moment when Jesus said for the first time, 'This is My Body,' there were two substantial presences of His one preexisting unchanged Body: the first natural, durable, under its proper appearances, and therefore local; the other derived, sacramental, temporary, under borrowed appearances and therefore not local—let us say by mode of pure substance."[82]

At each subsequent celebration of the Eucharist after Christ's resurrection and ascension, Christ's sacramental, substantial presence is that of his glorified bodily existence in heaven. Christ's body and blood are accompanied (*concomitari*) by all that is really associated with them in his everlasting glorified state: in virtue of Christ's human nature, his human soul, and in virtue of the hypostatic union, the divinity of the Logos. This concomitance includes also the body of Christ in relation to the blood present under the appearance (*species*) of wine, and the blood of Christ in relation to the body present under the appearance (*species*) of bread. Through real concomitance, because of the integral subsistence of the risen Christ in heaven, nothing less than the whole person of Christ is in the Eucharist. Because Thomas is absolutely unequivocal about this matter, it is worth citing him at length:

It is absolutely necessary to confess according to Catholic faith that the entire Christ is in this sacrament. Yet we must know that there is something of Christ in this sacrament in a twofold manner: first, as it were, by the power of the sacrament; secondly, from natural concomitance. By the power of the sacrament, there is under the species of this sacrament that into which the pre-existing substance of the bread and wine is changed, as expressed by the words of the form, which are effective in this as in the other sacraments; for instance, by the words—*This is My body*, or *This is My blood*. But from natural concomitance there is also in this sacrament that which is really united with that thing wherein the aforesaid conversion is terminated. For if any two things be really united, then wherever the one is really, there must the other also be: since things really united together are only distinguished by an operation of the mind.[83]

As the body, blood, soul, and divinity of Christ are really united and are distinguished from each other only by an operation of the human mind, it would be theologically misguided from the very outset to drive a wedge—and thus create a false dichotomy—between the *substantial* and the *personal* presence of Christ in the sacrament. The presence in the sacrament of the substance of Christ's body and the substance of Christ's blood entails by way of real concomitance the real substantial presence of Christ's undiminished humanity, body and soul; and the real presence of the undiminished substance of Christ's humanity, in virtue of its hypostatic union with the divine Word, entails the personal presence of the Logos.[84] Hence, all that is intrinsic to Christ's personhood in virtue of the incarnation (his undiminished concrete humanity, body and soul) as well as all that is constitutive of his personhood in virtue of the divine Sonship (the subsistent Trinitarian relations) is present in the sacrament.

On the basis of the principle of real concomitance, Thomas holds that after the consecration the whole Christ is contained under each appearance (*species*) of the sacrament, but differently in each case. Under the appearance (*species*) of the wine, by the power of the sacrament, only the substance of Christ's blood is present, and in virtue of real concomitance, his body, soul, and divinity. Under the appearance (*species*) of the bread, by the power of the sacrament, only the substance of his body is present, and in virtue of real concomitance his blood, soul, and divinity.

The explanatory power of the categories substance and quantity becomes evident when, in q. 76, a. 3, Thomas discusses how the whole Christ can be entirely under every part of the species of bread and wine.[85] The second objection of a. 3 conveys the full force of the issue at stake. It draws out clearly what the real presence of the concrete physical nature of Christ's body entails:

> Since Christ's is an organic body, it has parts determinately distant; for a determinate distance of the individual parts from each other is of the very nature of an organic body, as that of eye from eye, and eye from ear. But this could not be so, if Christ were entire under every part of the species; for every part would have to be under every other part, and so where one part would be, there another part would be. It cannot be then that the entire Christ is under every part of the host or of the wine contained in the chalice.[86]

In his response, Thomas properly extends his use of the principle of real concomitance. By the power of the sacrament, the substance of Christ's body is in the sacrament; by the power of real concomitance, the dimensive quantity of Christ's body is also there—the latter, as we came to understand earlier, being indispensable for the proper constitution of a material substance. Consequently, Christ's body is in this sacrament after the manner of substance (*per modum substantiae*), that is, "not after the manner of dimensions, which means, not in the way in which the dimensive quantity of a body is under the dimensive quantity of a place."[87] The glorious body of the risen Christ preexists and remains unchanged now in heaven under its proper appearances. His sacramental presence is real and directly and purely substantial under the postconsecratory appearances (*species*) of bread and wine. Hence, the risen Lord, who sits at the right hand of the Father in glory, is substantially present under the postconsecratory species without any change taking place in himself, but only in virtue of the substantial conversion into the substance of his body. In other words, after the Eucharistic consecration, Christ is neither bilocating nor multilocating; rather, the postconsecratory species are indicating many substantial presences of the one Christ in heaven. Christ's Eucharistic presence is nonlocal by way of substance. Thanks to the postconsecratory species and their dimensions that "circumscribe" the substantial presence of Christ, "the Eucharistic presence is, in fact, a presence of Christ's Body *in* a place, but not *by way* of place or dimension."[88]

The explanatory power of the metaphysical principle of substance and its ontological precedence in relation to all the accidents, including dimensive quantity, carries Thomas's response. Let us consider his response to the second objection:

> The determinative distance of parts in an organic body is based upon its dimensive quantity; but the nature of substance precedes even dimensive quantity. And since the conversion of the substance of the bread is terminated at the substance of the body of Christ, and since according to the manner of substance the body of Christ is properly and directly in this sacrament; such distance of parts is indeed in Christ's true body, which, however, is not compared to this sacrament according to such distance, but according to the manner of its substance.[89]

In an additional step that deepens his argument, Thomas shows how we can understand that indeed the whole dimensive quantity of Christ's body is in the sacrament. We find the crucial axiom he applies already in q. 76, a. 4, s.c.: "The existence of the dimensive quantity of any body cannot be separated from the existence of its substance. But in this sacrament the entire substance of Christ's body is present.... Therefore, the entire dimensive quantity of Christ's body is in this sacrament."[90] In his response, Thomas draws upon the by now familiar distinction between what is present by the power of the sacrament (*ex vi sacramenti*) and what is present according to real concomitance (*secundum realem concomitantiam*). By the power of the sacrament, the conversion is terminated at the substance of Christ's body and not at the dimensions of the body for, after all, the dimensive quantity of the bread clearly remains after the consecration. Applying the axiom of the *sed contra* that the existence of the dimensive quantity of any body cannot be separated from its substance, Thomas then adds the following: "Nevertheless, since the substance of Christ's body is not really deprived of its dimensive quantity and its other accidents, hence it comes that by reason of real concomitance the whole dimensive quantity of Christ's body and all its other accidents are in this sacrament."[91] In the response to the first objection he puts this decisive point even more succinctly:

> Since, then, the substance of Christ's body is present on the altar by the power of this sacrament, while its dimensive quantity is there concomitantly and as it were accidentally, therefore the dimensive quantity of Christ's body is in this sacrament, not according to its proper manner (namely, that the whole is in the whole, and the individual parts in individual parts), but after the manner of substance [*per modum substantiae*], whose nature is for the whole to be in the whole, and the whole to be in every part.[92]

The presence of the dimensive quantity of Christ's body after the manner of substance (*per modum substantiae*) is possible because dimensive quantity is intrinsic to material substance. While the substantial form is necessarily the form and thus the *actus* (act) of the whole as well as of every part and thereby constitutive of the unity of the whole material substance, dimensive quantity inheres in the matter of the substance establishing the order of distinguishable parts as a whole and in relation to the place. *Hence, in order for dimensive quantity to be present after the manner of substance, it does not require what is characteristic of dimensive quantity when it is realized according to its proper manner, namely, the relation to the place.* In q. 76, a. 5, co., Thomas gives a fuller description of dimensive quantity realized according to its proper manner: "Every body occupying a place is in the place according to the manner of dimensive quantity, namely, inasmuch as it is commensurate with the place according to its dimensive quantity."[93] And it is quite obvious that according to the proper manner of dimensive quantity it is impossible for two proper dimensive quantities naturally to be in the same subject at the same time— the proper dimensive quantity of Christ's body and blood and the proper dimensive quantity of bread and wine. However, "the place in which Christ's body is, is not empty; nor yet is it properly filled with the substance of Christ's body, which is not there locally ... but it is filled with the sacramental species, which have to fill the place either because of the nature of dimensions, or at least miraculously, as they also subsist miraculously after the fashion of substance."[94]

At the same time, it is possible after the conversion for the dimensive quantity of the species of bread to remain commensurate with the place it occupies while the dimensive quantity of Christ's body is present after the manner of substance (*per modum substantiae*): "The accidents of Christ's body are in this sacrament by real concomitance [*secundum realem concomitantiam*]. And therefore, those accidents of Christ's body which are intrinsic to it are in this sacrament. But to be in a place is an accident when compared with the extrinsic container. And therefore, it is not necessary for Christ to be in this sacrament as in a place."[95] The remaining accidents of bread and wine after the Eucharistic consecration account for the fact that Christ's body is indeed related to a particular place, that is, precisely to the place where the postconsecratory appearances (*species*) of bread and wine are located. That dimensive quantity that remains after the Eucharistic consecration is the selfsame quantity that had caused the preconsecratory Eucharistic species, bread and wine, to be individuated and located in the first place. Hence, the dimensive quantity of the preconsecratory species of bread and wine serves after the consecration as a medium for all the other accidents that previously belonged to the preconsecratory Eucharistic species of bread and wine. Thomas conceives of the Eucharistic conversion as a kind of succession, similar to the succession that occurs in creation *ex nihilo*, where being simply succeeds nonbeing. Analogous to the succession from nonbeing to being in creation *ex nihilo*, in Eucharistic conversion the body of Christ—already existing in heaven—begins to exist on the altar under the postconsecratory appearance (*species*) of the bread, that is, under its remaining accident of dimensive quantity and under all the other accidents (quality, place etc.) that remain by way of the bread's dimensive quantity.[96]

The metaphysics of material substance as Thomas receives and develops it establishes a real distinction at the heart of dimensive quantity. Recall that dimensive quantity inheres in the matter of the substance. While the substantial form is the *actus* that realizes the whole, the parts, and the unity of the parts as a whole, dimensive quantity realizes (1) the order of distinguishable parts as a whole, that is, the distinct structure of the whole material substance, and (2) the relation to the place. Dimensive quantity thus has two formal effects that are really distinct from each other, the *primary* formal effect, the order of distinguishable parts as a whole (*ordo partium in toto*), and the *secondary* formal effect, the order of the parts in the place (*ordo partium in loco*). Because it is a real and not merely a conceptual distinction, the primary formal effect of dimensive quantity may be realized without its secondary formal effect also being realized. This important distinction enables later generations of Thomists to argue that even under the postconsecratory appearances (*species*) of bread and wine, it is by way of the primary formal effect of quantity that the substance of Christ's body and blood is really present in its concrete particularity as this individual substance. I shall now briefly consider why this important distinction—implicit in Thomas's own teaching—is made explicit and put to quite extensive use in the school of Thomism.

CONCEPTUAL DEVELOPMENTS
IN THE THOMIST SCHOOL

The main reason for eventually making explicit a distinction that was implicit in Thomas's own teaching was the need to develop a more nuanced and differentiated response to the question of how one can account metaphysically for the possibility that dimensive quantity subsists solely after the manner of substance (*per modum substantiae*). This development occurred in part in response to an intense debate after Thomas's death about the nature of quantity primarily among Franciscan theologians. The Franciscan theologian Peter John Olivi (1248–98) challenged the view held by both Bonaventure and Thomas that transubstantiation indeed was the only rationally satisfying metaphysical account for Christ's real, corporeal presence in the Eucharist and that all remaining accidents in a material substance are subjected to quantity. The accounts of Peter John Olivi, John Duns Scotus (ca. 1266–1308), and William of Ockham (1285–1347) form unfinished pieces of an alternative account of real presence. This debate offers an instructive case study for the kinds of metaphysical objections that can be raised against the Thomist position—and the ensuing significant and, indeed, grave metaphysical conundrums that such an alternative metaphysical account faces.

From a properly theological perspective, however, this debate simply represents a path not taken by the church's tradition. For the one crucial point that Olivi, Scotus, and Ockham agree upon in their accounts of real presence is that substantial conversion is not what accounts for Christ's real presence. But this position was not accepted by the church's tradition. On the contrary, without explicitly endorsing the Thomist metaphysical account of real presence, the Council of Trent essentially affirmed the position jointly held by Bonaventure and Thomas, namely, that it is indeed substantial conversion that accounts for Christ's real, corporeal presence in the Eucharist.[97]

Hence, unfolding the implicit entailments of Thomas's teaching became necessary in light of different philosophical accounts that gave rise to variant theological doctrines in the centuries after Thomas's death. These philosophical accounts in one way or another would identify substance itself with its property of quantitative extension and, consequently, strongly compromised the genuine, whole presence of the dimensive quantity of Christ's body.

The late medieval school of the *via moderna*—largely indebted to the thought of William of Ockham and eventually identified by its opponents simply as the "nominalists" (*Nominales*)—came to regard material substance to be extended *per se* and not as informed by the "first" or "absolute" accident of quantity. For Ockham there is no real distinction between substance and quantity. Quantity, rather, has a purely nominal status; that is, quantity is a connotative term that stands for substance in its aspect of extension.[98] Consequently,

Ockham has to explain how after the consecration, the substance of Christ's body becomes present without being *quanta*, without parts outside of parts and the consequent natural order of parts (*ordo partium*). This is his solution: because the notion "quantity" simply connotes substance, it can be removed without any real change in the underlying subject. And so, while the connotative notion of quantity is removed, Christ's body is nevertheless definitively present under the host and each of its parts. Hence, the natural parts of Christ's body have to interpenetrate each other and, consequently, the natural order of parts (*ordo partium*) is dissolved. From the point of view of Thomas's teaching, the Ockhamist position fails to maintain the integrity of the dimensive quantity of Christ's body in the sacrament and consequently fails to make explicit the presence of the whole Christ in the sacrament.[99]

To consider the second major catalyst for the Thomist school's explication of Thomas's teaching, we need to advance from the fourteenth century to the seventeenth, from Ockham to Descartes. While substance was a key notion in René Descartes's swiftly spreading philosophy, the notion underwent a profound transmutation in his doctrine. Inspired by the clarity and certainty of mathematics, Descartes searched for a new philosophy whose foremost criterion was the clarity and distinctness of ideas. Disregarding—in a not altogether unproblematic way—the long tradition of metaphysical inquiry on this matter, he defined substance as a thing that exists in such a way that it needs no other thing for its existence. In light of this criterion, he identified two kinds of substance: one intellectual, the other material. Thought constitutes the nature of the intellectual substance, and spatial extension (length, breadth, depth) the nature of corporeal substance.[100] The consequent identification in reality of substance and quantity does not come as a surprise. In his *Principles of Philosophy* he states: "There is no real difference between quantity and the extended substance; the difference is merely a conceptual one, like that between number and the thing which is numbered."[101] In this particular work of Descartes, one sees clearly the shift from a metaphysical consideration of the principles of reality as modes of being to a philosophical analysis of conceptions or ideas understood as mental images. Such a transformation of metaphysical principles of being into univocal mental conceptions guided by the criterion of "ocular clarity" leads unavoidably to the loss of the metaphysical principle of substance itself in relationship to the accidents, and with it, to a profound lack of understanding of the nature and function of categories, as well as of the real distinction between substance and quantity in a sensible thing.[102]

Cartesian theologians, especially in France and Italy, began to apply this deceptively simple but indeed radically changed notion of substance to the doctrine of Eucharistic conversion.[103] According to Descartes's new understanding of corporeal substance, Christ's substantial presence in the sacrament is conceived in the following way: after the consecration, the dimensive quantity of the bread and the wine cannot remain (and with it none of the other accidents of bread and wine), for two corporeal substances cannot, of course, occupy the same space at the same time. According to the Cartesian theologians, what is present after the consecration is nothing but the glorious body of Christ *per se*. In order to veil the surpassing holiness of Christ's bodily presence and also in order not to deter the faithful from communion, God provides the sensible effects of bread and wine to the sensory organs. According to a different view defended by other Cartesian theologians, it is Christ's body that provides the sensible effects of bread and wine by taking on new surfaces similar to those of bread and wine. Furthermore, the Cartesian theologians hold that in virtue of being a corporeal substance, after the consecration Christ's body has to be locally extended. Consequently, by way of some mode of contraction or condensation it must be reduced to the circumscriptive extension of what has the visual appearance of a host or wine in a chalice.

In light of these alternative positions, one can begin to appreciate in hindsight the profundity of Thomas's teaching that the dimensive quantity of Christ is in the sacrament by way of natural concomitance after the manner of substance. In view of the alternative accounts of the real presence of Christ advanced by the nominalist school and later the Cartesian school, the Thomist school advanced its metaphysical investigation. By way of extrapolating Thomas's metaphysical principles, Thomist theologians inquired how it is possible and what it means for dimensive quantity to be present by way of natural concomitance after the manner of substance. The Thomist school advanced three central developments of Thomas's thought. (1) Because there is a real distinction between the principles of substance and quantity, material substance requires quantity as its absolute first accident. (2) Because local extension presupposes some distinction of parts from other parts, it is possible to distinguish between the essence of quantity (which is to have a formal structure of parts that are different from other parts, i.e., "outside of other parts") and the specific property of quantity (which is local extension). The Thomist commentators identified the essence of quantity as the formal structure (*ratio formalis*) or the *primary formal effect of quantity*. It is the order of distinguishable parts as a whole (*ordo partium in toto*). They identified the specific property of quantity as the *secondary formal effect of quantity*, which is the order of the parts in place (*ordo partium in loco*) and with it the position or situation of the parts under consideration relative to other parts in space (*ubi et situs*). Although they are logically distinct, under normal conditions, these two formal effects of quantity do not occur separately in nature. (3) Substance as such is indivisible and hence a substantial form or a separate substance (angel) has no capacity of local extension. Every material substance, however, has intrinsically—that is, in virtue of being a material substance—parts that are different from and hence outside of other parts, as well as a specific order among the parts, and consequently the capacity to be divided into parts and to be locally extended.

As a co-constitutive principle of material substance quantity is really distinct from substance. Yet in reality the essence of quantity is inseparable from a material substance. For quantity is the "first" or "absolute" accident of material substance. In a material substance's normal, locally extended existence, its dimensive quantity always presupposes the essence of quantity, which exists after the manner of substance (*per modum substantiae*). That is, the existence of a material substance as extended in space presupposes the distinction of parts from other parts and the intrinsic (though not yet locally realized) order between these parts as a necessary accident of material substance. Hence it is not intrinsically impossible for what is ontologically a distinct (though not independent) principle of the constitution of material substances to subsist solely after the manner of substance (*per modum substantiae*) simply in virtue of immediate divine causality, with God as first cause substituting directly proper secondary causality. All that a miracle presupposes is the absence of logical impossibility.

In unfolding one aspect of Thomas's teaching in this particular way, the Thomist school was able to maintain (against the nominalist position) that the *whole* Christ, including his dimensive quantity, is in the sacrament after the manner of substance, and (against the Cartesian position) that the Eucharistic species maintain their properly realized dimensive quantity in their local space, while Christ's body has its properly realized quantitative dimension in Christ's glorified state in heaven alone.

In summary: according to the Thomist commentators, the primary formal effect of quantity specifies the order of distinguishable parts as a whole (*ordo partium in toto*). This order (which is the essence of quantity) gives rise to a really distinct determination, the secondary formal effect of quantity, which is the order of one part to another (*ordo relationis*) and with it the order of the parts in place (*ordo partium in loco*). The order of the parts in place denotes the position or situation of the parts relative to other parts in space (*ubi et situs*).[104] Because the order of distinguishable parts as a whole (*ordo partium in toto*) can be considered indeterminately, the primary formal effect of dimensive quantity is logically separable from its secondary formal effect. And consequently, the primary formal effect of dimensive quantity and its secondary formal effect are separable according to their modes of being.

SUMMARY

At this point, we can identify two vital results of this account of the categories of substance and quantity in the teaching of Thomas and the Thomist tradition. First, substance is not a mere conceptual name in the modern, nominalist sense. On the contrary, substances denote entities that subsist in their own existence—"therefore only substances are properly and truly called beings" (*unde solae substantiae proprie et vere dicuntur entia*).[105] Substances address the intellect and are formally received by it.

Second, Thomas's teaching on material substance allows for the real distinction between the primary formal effect of quantity, the order of distinguishable parts as a whole (*ordo partium in toto*), and its secondary formal effect, the order of the parts in place (*ordo partium in loco*). That is, even under the postconsecratory appearances (*species*) of bread and wine, it is by way of the primary formal effect of quantity that the substance of Christ's body and blood is really present in concrete particularity as *this* individual substance. This substantial presence, however, emphatically does not pertain to the order of the parts in place (*ordo partium in loco*), nor to the position or situation of the parts under consideration relative to other parts in space (*ubi et situs*).[106] The substance of Christ's body and blood are present without deficiency of substance (which includes the primary formal effect of quantity, the order of distinguishable parts as a whole in relation to each other).

At the same time, after the consecration, the appearances (*species*) of bread and wine maintain their proper dimensive quantity, that is, their specific order of the parts in place (*ordo partium in loco*), as sustained by the primary formal effect of the quantity of bread and the quantity of wine. And because quantity is not identical with substance, the logical separability of the two allows for the possibility that the primary (*ordo partium in toto*) and the secondary (*ordo partium in loco*) formal effects of quantity are sustainable without the substance in which quantity inheres.[107] As all the other accidents inhere in substance by way of dimensive quantity, their sustainability is consequent upon the separate sustainability of the two effects of dimensive quantity.[108]

What difference does this distinction make? Consider the following argument advanced by Sylvester of Ferrara, the profound commentator on Thomas's *Summa contra Gentiles* concerning Thomas's discussion of how the body of Christ (as a proper material substance) can be in multiple places. Here is Thomas's text from *Summa contra Gentiles* IV.64.5: "The body of Christ in His own dimensions exists in one place only, but through the mediation of the dimensions of the bread passing into it its places are as many as there are places in which this sort of conversion is celebrated. For it is not divided into parts, but is entire in every single one; every consecrated bread is converted into the entire body of Christ."[109]

Sylvester of Ferrara, commenting on this text, advances a succinct version of the distinction between the two effects of quantity:

The effect of quantity is twofold. The one effect is completely intrinsic to that which has quantity [as it pertains to the *metaphysical order* of the constitution of a material substance], that is, quantification [*esse quantum*], divisibility into parts, and the order of parts as a whole. The other effect is in some manner extrinsic [as it pertains to the *physical order* of material substances relating *qua* quantity to other material substances], namely, insofar as quantity pertains to the thing in the outward order, that is, insofar as it corresponds to another distinguishable quantity, and the parts of the one correspond to the location of the parts of the other quantity. The first effect is necessarily and per se proper to quantity. The second effect, however, pertains to quantity only if it is ordered principally and per se to a place and toward extrinsic dimensions. Consequently, in the sacrament of the altar, the quantity of Christ's body, existing under the dimensions of the bread, has the first effect. For the body of Christ is in itself divisible and has an order of parts as a whole. It does not, however, have the second effect. For the parts of Christ's body do not correspond to the dimensive parts of the bread nor to the location of these parts, but the whole is under whatsoever part. Consequently, it can be said that the body of Christ is under the dimensions of the bread in a divisible as well as an indivisible way: divisible insofar as it has in and of itself divisible parts; indivisible, however, because its parts do not correspond to the parts of those dimensions, but rather the whole corresponds to whatsoever part, similar to the way the soul as a whole is in each part [of the body].[110]

Sylvester of Ferrara's commentary allows us to see with greater clarity what indeed is entailed in Thomas's own teaching. If Christ's words, "This is my body, this is my blood," are to be taken at face value and not as spiritual or metaphorical flights from reality, the proper metaphysical avenue available to the *intellectus fidei* is material substance as inherently modified by quantity. Instead of diminishing or "reifying" the *mysterium fidei*, this kind of rigorous metaphysical contemplation lets the *mysterium* shine forth in its consummate glory.

POPE PAUL VI'S *MYSTERIUM FIDEI* (1965)

At this point we must turn to two central sections of Pope Paul VI's encyclical letter *Mysterium Fidei*: first, its explicit reaffirmation of the decree of Trent, and second, its own extrapolation from it:

The Council of Trent, basing itself on this faith of the Church, "openly and sincerely professes that after the consecration of the bread and wine, Our Lord Jesus Christ, true God and man, is really, truly, and substantially contained in the Blessed Sacrament of the Holy Eucharist under the outward appearances of sensible things."[111] And so Our Savior is present in His humanity not only in His natural manner of existence at the right hand of the Father, but also at the same time in the sacrament of the Eucharist "in a manner of existing that we can hardly express in words but that our minds, illumined by faith, can come to see as possible to God and that we must most firmly believe."[112] ... To avoid any misunderstanding of this type of presence, which goes beyond the laws of nature and constitutes the greatest miracle of its kind,[113] we have to listen with docility to the voice of the teaching and praying Church. Her voice, which constantly echoes the voice of Christ, assures us that the way in which Christ becomes present in this Sacrament is through the conversion of the whole substance of the bread into His body and of the whole substance of the wine into His blood, a unique and truly wonderful conversion that the Catholic Church fittingly and properly calls transubstantiation.[114] As a result of transubstantiation, the species of bread and wine undoubtedly take on a new signification and a new finality, for they are no longer ordinary bread and wine but instead a sign of something sacred and a sign of spiritual food; but they take on this new signification, this new finality, precisely because they contain a new "reality" which we can rightly call ontological. For what now lies beneath the aforementioned species is not what was there before, but something completely different; and not just in the estimation of Church belief but in reality, since once the substance or nature of the bread and wine has been changed into the body and blood of Christ, nothing remains of the bread and the wine except for the species—beneath which Christ is present whole and entire in His physical "reality," corporeally present, although not in the manner in which bodies are in a place. (pars. 45–46)

In order to receive this teaching according to the highest degree of its intelligibility, contemporary dogmatic theology, conceived as sacred theology or holy teaching (*sacra doctrina*), would do well to receive and reconsider Thomas's metaphysical analysis of (1) substance and quantity, (2) the nonidentity of substance and quantity as modes of being, (3) dimensive quantity as the immediately inherent accident of material substance, and especially (4) the real distinction and hence the possible separability of the primary formal effect of quantity, the order of distinguishable parts as a whole (*ordo partium in toto*), from its secondary formal effect, the order of the parts in place (*ordo partium in loco*). Furthermore, (5) it is Thomas—felicitously assisted by the Thomist commentators—who helps us understand why, in considering the conversion of one material substance into another material substance, it is impossible to disregard dimensive quantity.[115] It is indeed the latter—or more precisely and properly considered, its primary formal effect—that, under present intellectual conditions, can greatly assist in keeping substantial, corporeal presence from sliding into a mere metaphor of some atmospheric presence in general. "For," as John of St. Thomas avers in his succinct summary of Thomas's teaching, "once quantity is removed, substance lacks integral parts that are ordered formally by reason of the part and hence distinguishable."[116] Last but not least, (6) Thomas shows that because of real concomitance, Christ's surpassing personal presence in the Eucharist has its indispensable anchor in the substantial presence of his body and his blood under the Eucharistic species. For, according to Thomas, nothing less and nothing more than Christ's very humanity constitutes God's surpassingly efficacious instrument for the salvation of humanity.[117]

Most arresting in *Mysterium Fidei*, with its very precise and nuanced distinctions and demarcations, is undoubtedly the fact that it advances sufficient conceptual specificity to encourage and invite further metaphysical contemplation of the *mysterium fidei* along the lines of Thomas and also, if necessary under particular intellectual conditions, of the classical Thomist tradition.[118] For the presence *par excellence*, the substantial presence of Christ, as the result of the conversion of the whole substance of bread and wine into Christ's body and blood, seems to require nothing less than the very presence of the specific order of distinguishable parts as a whole (*ordo partium in toto*) of Christ's precious body and blood, "contained in the Blessed Sacrament of the Holy Eucharist under the outward appearances" of bread and wine.[119]

4

"This Is My Body"

Faith Preserves the Intellect
from Deception

Lest the Thomist deployment of substance becomes seriously lop-sided, that is, incorrectly received as a kind of crude, nonsacramental realism, I must now turn to the theological context into which Thomas squarely places his doctrine of Eucharistic conversion—the antecedent context of sacramental signification and causation—and even one step back to the very root of sacramental signification as well as causation: Christ's passion on the cross. For Thomas maintains that "the power of Christ's Passion is united to us by faith and the sacraments, but in different ways; because the link that comes from faith is produced by an act of the soul; whereas the link that comes from the sacraments is produced by making use of exterior things."[120] According to Thomas:

It is manifest ... that Christ delivered us from our sins principally through His Passion, not only by way of efficiency and merit, but also by way of satisfaction. Likewise by His Passion He inaugurated the Rites of the Christian Religion by offering Himself—"an oblation and a sacrifice to God" [Eph 5:2]. Wherefore it is manifest that the sacraments of the Church derive their power especially from Christ's Passion, the virtue of which is in a manner united to us by our receiving the sacraments. It was in sign of this that from the side of Christ hanging on the Cross there flowed water and blood, the former of which belongs to Baptism, the latter to the Eucharist, which are the principal sacraments.[121]

This use of exterior things as an instrumental extension of Christ's humanity, which is itself an instrument of his divinity, constitutes, in Abbot Vonier's apposite words in his *A Key to the Doctrine of the Eucharist*, "the sacramental world." In Thomas's understanding, the sacraments substitute for Christ and extend his work. As such, they are both cause and sign; they are essentially signs that are inherently causal. Hence, they effect what they signify.[122] In other words, every sacrament is a sign, but "a sign of an efficaciousness."[123] The Eucharistic mystery sits at the very heart of this sacramental world in which signs are inherently causal. And the sign-character of the sacrament is crucial. Vonier emphatically stresses that

at no time in the eucharistic mystery do we deal with Christ in His natural condition, *in propria specie.* . . . He must be there *in specie aliena*—in a condition different from His natural one—in order to safeguard the character of the sacrament as a sign. . . . His Presence in the sacrament must be truly such that at no time could it be seen otherwise than by the eye of faith.[124]

Abbot Vonier's point is absolutely essential. By way of this theological insight, Thomas provides the proper *sacramental* context necessary to understand the true presence. By contrast, two centuries before Thomas, the concept of true presence was discussed at the Synod of Rome presided over by Pope Nicholas II in 1069. Berengar of Tours (ca. 999–1088), arguably France's most brilliant theologian of the eleventh century, had adopted the teaching of the Frankish monk Ratramnus (d. ca. 870) on a purely spiritual presence without a substantial change in the elements. A correction of this teaching was the central topic of the Synod of Rome. Cardinal Humbert of Silva Candida drafted a formula to be signed by Berengar. In this formula, one section maintains that after the consecration not only the sacrament but also the true body and blood of Christ are *sensibly* (not only in the sacrament, but also in truth) touched and broken by the priest and crushed by the teeth of the faithful.[125] This section is interestingly not repeated in the later formulas of submission to Pope St. Gregory VII that Berengar had to sign in 1078 and 1079. (It is the later formula that is cited in Paul VI, *Mysterium Fidei*, par. 52.) Berengar's spiritualism and the physicalism of Cardinal Hubert of Silva Candida's suppressed section from the formula of confession are two equally erroneous theological reductions of the mystery of Christ's real presence. Thomas's profound understanding of the *sui generis* sacramental order and its own proper efficacy by way of instrumental causality significantly deepened and helpfully clarified the theological reception of the *mysterium fidei*.[126]

In unfolding the various aspects characteristic of this *sui generis* sacramental order, Thomas employs a set of distinctions, somewhat established by his time, that developed in a complex process of patristic and early medieval theological discourse: *sacramentum tantum*, the sign only; *res et sacramentum*, the thing and the sign; *res tantum*, the thing only. The first, the sign only (*sacramentum tantum*), comprises a sacramental form and sacramental matter. The form is the priest's act of consecrating the bread and wine (that is, the priest's speaking of the words of consecration over bread and wine with the intent to consecrate this bread and wine). The sacramental matter is the bread and wine. The second, the thing and the sign (*res et sacramentum*), refers to the body and blood of Christ substantially present at the term of the Eucharistic conversion. Now, this is called "thing and sign" (*res et sacramentum*), because it is both the thing (*res*) which is signified by the sacramental sign (*sacramentum tantum*), namely, Christ's true body and blood, and a sign. For Christ's substantial presence points beyond itself and signifies in turn the thing itself (*res tantum*), that is, the spiritual effect of the Eucharist, which is the specific sacramental grace of further incorporation into the mystical body of Christ, the perfect union of charity between the head and the body.[127] Hence, the pivotal middle term of the three sacramental terms, *res et sacramentum*, indicates the crucial double signification that occurs in the Eucharist: first, the reality of Christ's substantial, corporeal presence is signified by the *sacramentum tan-*

tum, the species of bread and wine; and, secondly, the very reality of Christ's substantial, corporeal presence itself signifies (therefore *res et sacramentum*) the spiritual effects of Eucharistic communion. The *sacramentum tantum* and the *res et sacramentum* jointly signify and effect the *res tantum*; the dynamic process of the sacramental act is cumulative.[128] Because the whole order of sacramental grace derives from the power of Christ's passion on the cross, the thing and the sign (*res et sacramentum*), as Abbot Vonier rightly stresses, "also signifies sacrifice, as being the immediate representation of Christ immolated on the Cross."[129] The hurried reader of the *Summa Theologiae* might easily miss where Thomas addresses this important matter in the context of accounting for the whole Christ being entirely present under the two postconsecratory species of bread and wine:

> Although the whole Christ is under each species, yet it is so not without purpose. For in the first place this serves to represent Christ's Passion, in which the blood was separated from the body; hence in the form for the consecration of the blood mention is made of its shedding. Secondly, it is in keeping with the use of this sacrament, that Christ's body be shown apart to the faithful as food, and the blood as drink. Thirdly, it is in keeping with its effect, in which sense it was stated above [*ST* III, q. 74, a. 1] that "the body is offered for the salvation of the body, and the blood for the salvation of the soul."[130]

In virtue of its sacramental representation, the Eucharistic sacrifice presents—makes present without repeating—Christ's sacrifice on the cross of Golgotha.[131] Because of the comprehensive sacramental representation, the sacrificial dimension of the Eucharist exists not only at the level of the *res et sacramentum*, but also at the level of the *sacramentum tantum* (e.g., separate consecrations) and at the level of the *res tantum* (the end or the fruit of Christ's sacrifice are the many grains of wheat making up the one bread, thus signifying the united mystical body of Christ).

Christ's Eucharistic presence occurs immediately with the *sacramental presentation* of his crucified humanity—the incarnate Son's utter self-giving to the Father in love, obedient to the point of death—his body and blood being sacramentally separated in the one sacrament. Is there a more abiding personal presence possible of Christ to the church in its state of pilgrimage (*in via*) than in the sacramental form of his perfect, final oblation to the Father on the cross (Eph 5:2; Heb 9:14)?

All of this is to say that in Thomas's doctrine of Eucharistic conversion, the substantial, corporeal presence of Christ in the Eucharist does not at all occlude or thwart the abiding *sacramental* signification of the Eucharistic species. The sign only (*sacramentum tantum*) with its proper instrumentality is in no way abolished by the Eucharistic conversion. On the contrary, the postconsecratory appearances (*species*) of bread and wine remain signs indicating the real substantial presence of Christ's body and blood. Recall that even under normal epistemic conditions, substantial being is not sensible.[132] While we perceive (see, hear, smell, or touch) a particular sensible unity, the substance of the sensible unity occurs to the intellect only, precisely because of the sensible experience. To be able to get to the point of a sensible experience is to get to its substance, that is, to penetrate to the essence of a thing. This very penetration to the essence of a thing is, according to Thomas, the specific task of the intellect, whose proper object is substance:

The word "intellect" suggests a *deeply penetrating* knowledge: the Latin word "*intelligere*" suggests "reading the interiors." And this is quite clear to anyone considering the difference between *intellect* and *sense*: for sense-knowledge has to do with *exterior sensible* qualities; whereas intellective knowledge penetrates right to the *essence* of the thing: for the object of the intellect is *what the thing is*.... Now, there are many sorts of things which are "hidden inside" [as it were], regarding which it is necessary that human knowledge "penetrate to the interior," so to speak. Thus, "*within*" the accidents lies hidden the substantial nature of the thing; "*within*" words lie hidden the meanings of words; "*within*" likenesses and symbols lie hidden the symbolized truth; and effects *lie hidden* in causes, and vice versa. Hence, with respect to all these cases, one can speak of "intellect."[133]

In assent to the dominical words, the faith-guided intellect recognizes that after the consecration the preconsecratory substances of bread and wine are absent. Directed by the dominical words, the intellect rather perceives the substance, Christ's body and blood, really present under the postconsecratory appearances (*species*) of bread and wine. Echoing his earlier teaching, Thomas reminds his readers at this very point of the general epistemic condition of human knowledge of a substance *qua* substance:

Substance, as such, is not visible to the bodily eye, nor does it come under any one of the senses, nor under the imagination, but solely under the intellect, whose object is *what a thing is*.... And therefore, properly speaking, Christ's body, according to the mode of being which it has in the sacrament, is perceptible neither by the sense nor by the imagination, but only by the intellect, which is called the spiritual eye.[134]

Accordingly, Thomas stresses that indeed "[Christ's body] can be seen by a wayfarer through faith alone [*sola fide*], like other supernatural things."[135]

Hence the character of the sacrament as a sign abides from beginning to end. It is by way of the instrumental causality inherent in sacramental signification that the sign only (*sacramentum tantum*) in its sacramental matter (bread and wine) and in its sacramental form (the priest speaking the words of consecration over bread and wine) constitutes the irreplaceable and indispensable starting point for the sacramental conversion. And after the consecration, the postconsecratory sacramental appearances (*species*) of bread and wine continue to carry the *sacramental* signification of the Eucharistic conversion. Consequently, there is no deception at all taking place in this sacrament. "For," as Thomas argues, "the accidents which are discerned by the senses are truly present. But the intellect, whose proper object is substance ... is preserved by faith from deception ... because faith is not contrary to the senses, but concerns things which sense does not reach."[136] Remember Thomas's definition of faith as "the act of believing," that is, "an act of the intellect assenting to the Divine truth at the command of the will moved by the grace of God."[137] Like any other act of assent, the assent of faith does not terminate in a proposition, but rather in a "thing," a "reality" (*res*).

"For," Thomas says, "as in science we do not form propositions, except in order to have knowledge about things through their means, so it is in faith."[138] In short, all true assents, be they of science or of faith, terminate in the reality made intelligible by the proposition formed. And the proper object of our intellect, our understanding, is "what a thing is" (*quid res est*), that is, its "quiddity" or substance. Thus, it is only by way of our intellect beholding the substance of a *res* that we can say what it is. For we name things as we know them.[139]

The thing (*res*) to which this particular truth of faith refers is recognized by way of hearing alone (*solo auditu*)—"this is my body" (*hoc est corpus meum*). The pronoun "this" (*hoc*) in the sacramental form "this is my body" is the epistemic key for the knowledge of faith. As Stephen Brock puts it lucidly: "What the pronoun stands for is 'that which is contained under these species, in general,' or, more precisely, 'the substance contained under the accidents,' which previously was bread, and afterwards is the body of Christ."[140] By the pronoun "this" (*hoc*) in the sacramental form "this is my body," the "obscure knowledge" of faith does occur, and it is the will that "uses such knowledge well, to wit, by assenting to unseen things because God says that they are true."[141] By giving assent to the divine truth, received by way of the dominical words, faith's obscure knowledge preserves the intellect from deception. It is by way of the eye of faith (whose gaze is, so to speak, directed by the will commanding the intellect to assent to the truth of the proposition "This is my body, this is my blood") that the intellect beholds obscurely the substance of Christ's body and blood and hence indeed beholds the truth, the objective truth of the sacrament. What the intellect beholds non-discursively by the eye of faith—which in this case is instructed *solo auditu*—can and indeed *must* be spelled out by the *intellectus fidei* in precise predicamental concepts.

To summarize: the intellect obscurely beholds Christ's substantial presence under the Eucharistic species, informed not by the senses, but by assenting to the divine truth *solo auditu* at the command of the will moved by the grace of God: thus the truth is given

to Christians (*dogma datur Christianis*). By directing the intellect to
the truth beyond the senses (a truth that in all its obscurity can indeed only be attained by the intellect), faith prevents the intellect
from falling into deception. As Thomas expressed it with unsurpass-
able clarity, simplicity, and beauty in his hymn *Adoro te devote*:

> Visus, tactus, gustus, in te fallitur;
> Sed auditu solo tuto creditur.
> Credo quidquid dixit Dei Filius.
> Nil hoc verbo veritatis verius.
>
> In cruce latebat sola Deitas;
> At hic latet simul et humanitas.
> Ambo tamen credens atque confitens
> Peto quod petivit latro poenitens.
>
> Sight and touch and taste here fail;
> Hearing only can be believed.
> I trust what God's own Son has said.
> Truth from truth is best received.
>
> Divinity, on the Cross, was hid;
> Humanity here comes not to thought.
> Believing and confessing both,
> I seek out what the Good Thief sought.[142]

Precisely because the truth is given to Christians through the
Word of truth himself and received in faith by hearing alone (*solo
auditu*), faith preserves the intellect from deception. For Thomas
there is a subtle but precise relationship between the doctrine of
faith and the metaphysical notion of substance. The intellect is preserved from deception by faith because, at the will's command, the
intellect assents to the doctrine of faith. Yet it is not a blind faith,
contra intellectum. Rather, the intellect beholds the truth of the doctrine of faith in its own proper and primordial channel of beholding and understanding reality by way of the intellect's own proper
object, substance. And the doctrine of faith as well as the truth that
substance conveys transcends the vagaries of history, the contexts of
culture and society, and the deliveries of the natural sciences. Hence,

we dare not jettison the metaphysical contemplation of the *intellectus fidei* as it arises from the basic, prephilosophical perception of the world, a metaphysical contemplation accessible—if not *de facto*, at least in principle—to all human beings.[143] For as after the consecration the intellect beholds through faith alone (*sola fide*) "what a thing is [*quod quid est*],"[144] that is, the very substance of Christ's body and blood under the Eucharistic species, the *intellectus fidei* properly understands what it beholds by way of the predicament substance (see appendix 4, below).

Eucharistic transubstantiation, as defended doctrinally and interpreted discursively with surpassing profundity and simplicity by Thomas Aquinas, is the hidden power that enables faith to preserve the intellect from deception and hence enables the intellect to "come along" and, by the eye of faith, in the very darkness of superintelligibility, to behold the hidden substance of Christ's body and blood and hence Christ's real presence in body, soul, and divinity. Such beholding, indeed, "belongs to the perfection of faith," for after all, Thomas argues, "since faith is of things unseen, as Christ shows us His Godhead invisibly, so also in this sacrament He shows us His flesh in an invisible manner."[145]

5

"You Are My Friends"

Christ's Eucharistic Presence, Central Token
of Christ's Surpassing Friendship

Finally, in order to consider the relationship between Christ's sacramental body (*res et sacramentum*) and Christ's mystical body (*res sacramenti*), it is opportune at this point briefly to revisit the opening article of *ST* III, q. 75. For here, as already mentioned above, Thomas reminds his readers that in the Gospel of John, Christ, the incarnate Logos, makes the startling statement to his disciples, "You are my friends" (Jn 15:14). And, as Aristotle had rightly realized, "It is the special feature of friendship to live together with friends," to share each other's presence.[146] So it is not really surprising that for Thomas, for whom friendship with God is, after all, the path of deification, the Eucharist is Christ's central token of surpassing friendship, the "sign of supreme charity."[147] For "yet meanwhile in our pilgrimage He does not deprive us of His bodily presence; but unites us with Himself in this sacrament through the truth of His body and blood."[148] Thomas cites John 6:56: "He who eats my flesh and drinks my blood abides in me, and I in him" (RSV). It should therefore not come as a surprise that Thomas regards the ensuing sacramental union of Christ with the faithful in the Eucharist—a surpassing abiding in each other—as the reality of the sacrament, the *res sacramenti*: "The reality of the sacrament is the unity of the mystical body."[149] The "thing" of the sacrament (*res sacramenti*), or better, the sacramental grace, is the mystical body of Christ. This sacramental grace is not automatically received by everyone who participates in the *sacramentum tantum* and receives the *res et sacramentum* physically, but is received only by those whose faith is informed by charity, that is, who, enabled by grace, intellectually and volitionally embrace the substantial, personal presence of the one whose body and blood they receive sacramentally. Christ's mystical body is united through Christ's sacramental body by way of the bond of charity that unites each member with the head.[150] And when charity is lost, which is the case while one is in mortal sin, the sacrament cannot be received without lying to the sacrament, that is, signifying that one is united with Christ in charity while one is actually in a state of alienation from God. As Thomas states clearly:

> Whoever receives this sacrament, expresses thereby that he is made one with Christ, and incorporated in His members; and this is done by living faith [that is, faith informed by charity], which no one has who is in mortal sin. And therefore it is manifest that whoever receives this sacrament while in mortal sin, is guilty of lying to this sacrament, and consequently of sacrilege, because he profanes the sacrament: and therefore he sins mortally.[151]

Hence it is clear that the unity of the mystical body ensues from the true, personal, though sacramental presence of Christ, the head, to whom each member is joined by faith and charity. And it is from the head that each member receives the Holy Spirit, who joins together all members. The Holy Spirit does this by infusing each member with the virtue of charity. Remember, it is charity alone that makes it possible in Eucharistic communion to receive the reality of the sacrament (*res sacramenti*). Hence, in virtue of the charity infused by the Holy Spirit and sustained and increased by Eucharistic communion, the head abides in the members and the members in the head such that the church is indeed the body of Christ.[152]

Thomas's ecclesiology as well as his Eucharistic doctrine remains a salutary safeguard against a profoundly problematic development that set in soon after Vatican II, a development anticipated and denounced by Henri de Lubac in his important work *Corpus Mysticum*. Referring to the fundamental desire of recovering the communal aspect of the Mass that was a driving part of the liturgical movement of the 1930s and 1940s, de Lubac feared the degeneration of such corporate aspirations into purely naturalist impulses:

Indeed there is always a risk of forgetting: it is not the human fact of gathering for the communal celebration of the mysteries, it is not the collective exaltation that an appropriate pedagogy succeeds in extracting from it that will ever in the very least bring about the unity of the members of Christ. This cannot come about without the remission of sins, the first fruit of the blood that was poured out. The memorial of the Passion, the offering to the heavenly Father, the conversion of the heart: these, therefore, are the totally interior realities without which we will never have anything but a caricature of the community that we seek. But the Eucharist does not offer us some human dream: it is a *mystery of faith*.[153]

Very much in contrast with the "decapitated body" which seems to be the sad but inevitable outcome of a number of recent ecclesiologies "from below," it is nothing but the real, substantial presence of the head that—by way of a mutual Eucharistic abiding of Christ in the faithful and the faithful in Christ—causes and sustains the unity among the members. Recall, the Eucharistic real presence of the *res et sacramentum* is objectively real whether or not it is recognized by observers and whether or not those observers accept it in faith and grace toward the attainment of the *res tantum*.[154] The Eucharist's "unifying function without the reality of the Presence could be only an illusion."[155] Hence, it is indeed the case that "the Eucharist makes the Church,"[156] and it is Eucharistic transubstantiation that renders unmistakably explicit that the Eucharist makes the church only because Christ makes the Eucharist. De Lubac explicitly affirms this relationship between cause and effect, between the Eucharist and the church, in the conclusion of his *Corpus Mysticum*:

Eucharistic realism and ecclesial realism: these two realisms support one another, each is the guarantee of the other. Ecclesial realism safeguards Eucharistic realism and the latter confirms the former.... Today, it is above all our faith in the "real presence," made explicit thanks to centuries of controversy and analysis, that introduces us to faith in the ecclesial body: effectively signified by the mystery of the Altar, the mystery of the Church has to share the same nature and the same depth. Among the ancients, the perspective was often inverted. The accent was habitually placed on the effect rather than on the cause. But the ecclesial realism to which they universally offer us the most explicit testimony is at the same time, and when necessary, the guarantee of their Eucharistic realism. This is because the cause has to be proportionate to its effect." [157]

It is noteworthy that Henri de Lubac, not at all unlike the presently neglected and derided neo-Thomist theologians, does not hesitate to draw upon a metaphysical principle to support and illuminate a theological truth.

In his unjustly forgotten but still greatly instructive and relevant *ressourcement* in the Fathers and the medieval doctors, *The Mysteries of Christianity*, Matthias Joseph Scheeben, the great and in many regards still unsurpassed Catholic theologian of the nineteenth century, grasped the intention of Thomas's Eucharistic doctrine with a remarkable profundity.[158] Scheeben rightly emphasizes the active role of the Holy Spirit in the mutual abiding that builds up the mystical body of Christ:

It was not only to give some sensible indication of His presence that Christ has attached the real union of His body with us to the condition of our partaking of the consecrated bread, as we might suppose if the union itself were to be purely spiritual in form. He had a much higher purpose in mind: to effect a union that would be not simply the presence of His body in ours or a contact between the two bodies, but would be an organic connection between them. That our bodies may be assumed into His body and become one with it by being united to it, He takes that substance which naturally can and does become one body with us, and changes it into His body by conversion. To fuse our bodies with His body by the fire of the Holy Spirit, He melts down the food proper to our body by that same fire and changes it into His own body.... That Christ might become a member and the head of our race, it was not enough for Him to assume a human nature like ours; He had to take His nature from the very midst of the race. Similarly, to perfect the organic bond which is to bind us to Him, He wills not merely to bring the substance of His body into contact with us, but to implant Himself in us, or rather us in Him; He wishes us to strike root in Him, just as He took root in our race at the Incarnation. This He does by changing into His body the food that nourishes our body; into this food and by means of it He inserts our body in Himself as a branch is engrafted on a vine.[159]

And whoever has ears to hear will indeed not fail to recognize the echo of Thomas's teaching, as well as that of Scheeben, resounding in *Ecclesia de Eucharistia*, par. 22:

Incorporation into Christ, which is brought about by Baptism, is constantly renewed and consolidated by sharing in the Eucharistic Sacrifice, especially by that full sharing which takes place in sacramental communion. We can say not only that *each of us receives Christ,* but also that *Christ receives each of us.* He enters into friendship with us: "You are my friends" (Jn 15:14). Indeed, it is because of him that we have life: "He who eats me will live because of me" (Jn 6:57). Eucharistic communion brings about in a sublime way the mutual "abiding" of Christ and each of his followers: "Abide in me, and I in you" (Jn 15:4).[160]

Even before the most profound request for the ongoing presence of the friend was uttered, Christ had already instituted the surpassing gift of himself and thus responded to our deepest Christian longing: "Stay with us, for it is toward evening and the day is now far spent" (Lk 24:29). May our eyes of faith be opened each time when the priest, *in persona Christi,* speaks the words of consecration, the words of consummate divine friendship, "This is my body, this is my blood." What more can we ask for? Christ remains with us under the sacramental species in the Eucharist until the sacramental species disappear. He remains with us so that our faith may constantly grow and our hope increasingly rest assured in the abiding presence and everlasting nature of Christ's consummate friendship with those who love him.

Appendixes

An important indicator that for Thomas Eucharistic real presence entails Eucharistic transubstantiation is found in his doctrinal commentary on the decretal *Firmiter*, a profession of faith formulated at Council Lateran IV in 1215. Thomas wrote this commentary during his Orvieto period (1261–65); its title is *Expositio super primam et secundam Decretalem ad archidiaconum Tudertinum*.[161] In its statement of faith, Lateran IV uses the participle for transubstantive change: "Transsubstantiatis pane in corpus et vino in sanguinem potestate divina." In English translation the complete sentence reads thus: "His Body and Blood are truly contained in the sacrament of the altar under the appearances of bread and wine, the bread being transubstantiated into the body by the divine power and the wine into the blood, to the effect that we receive from what is his what he has received from what is ours in order that the mystery of unity may be accomplished."[162]

In his doctrinal commentary, Thomas understands the statement of faith to determine three distinct truths of the Eucharistic sacrifice, the first regarding the *res* contained under the sacrament, the second regarding the way Christ's body begins to be present under the sacrament, and the third regarding the valid ministry of the sacrament. In a seamless manner his interpretation of the second asser-

tion, transubstantiation, flows directly from his interpretation of the
first assertion, real presence:

Regarding this sacrifice [the Council] determines three things. First, the
truth of the thing contained under the sacrament, when [the Council]
states: "His body and blood are truly contained in the sacrament of the
altar under the appearances of bread and wine." [The Council], however, says "truly" in order to exclude the error of those who say that in this
sacrament the body and the blood of Christ are not present really and in
truth, but only figuratively, or just as in a sign. Yet [the Council] says: "under the appearances of bread and wine" in order to exclude the error of
those who say that in the sacrament of the altar the substance of the bread
and the substance of Christ's body are simultaneously contained, which
goes against the word of the Lord who says, according to Luke 22:19: "This
is my body." For if it had been so [according to those who hold consub-
stantiation], it would have been necessary [for Christ] to say: "Here is my
body." In order therefore to show that in this sacrament the substance of
the bread and the wine does not remain, but only the appearances, that is,
the accidents without the subject, [the Council] states: "under the appearances of bread and wine."

   Secondly, [the Council] shows in what way the body of Christ begins
to be present under the sacrament, that is, by the fact that the substance
of the bread is miraculously converted into the substance of Christ's body
and the substance of the wine into the substance of his blood; and this
is what [the Council] states: "The bread being transubstantiated into the
body by the divine power and the wine into the blood in order that the
mystery of unity may be accomplished," that is, in order to celebrate the
sacrament that is the sign of the Church's unity. Then as a result, "we receive from what is his what he has received from what is ours." For in this
sacrament we receive indeed his body and his blood which the Son of God
has received from our nature.

The Latin original reads thus:

Circa quod sacrificium *tria* determinat. *Primo* quidem veritatem rei sub sacramento contentae, cum dicit: *Cuius corpus et sanguis in sacramento altaris sub speciebus panis et vini veraciter continentur.* Dicit autem *Veraciter,* ad
excludendum errorem quorundam qui dixerunt quod in hoc sacramento
non est corpus Christi secundum rei veritatem, sed solum secundum fig-
uram, sive sicut in signo. Dicit autem: *Sub speciebus panis et vini,* ad exclu-

dendum errorem quorundam qui dixerunt quod in sacramento altaris simul continetur substantia panis, et substantia corporis Christi; quod est contra verbum Domini dicentis, Luc. xxii, 19: *Hoc est corpus meum*. Esset enim secundum hoc dicendum magis: "Hic est corpus meum." Ut ergo ostendat quod in hoc sacramento non remanet substantia panis et vini, sed solum species, idest accidentia sine subiecto, dicit: *Sub speciebus panis et vini*.

Secundo ostendit quomodo corpus Christi incipiat esse sub sacramento, scilicet per hoc quod substantia panis convertitur miraculose in substantiam corporis Christi, et substantia vini in substantiam sanguinis; et hoc est quod dicit: *Transsubstantiatis pane in corpus et vino in sanguinem potestate divina, ad mysterium perficiendum unitatis*, idest ad celebrandum hoc sacramentum, quod est signum ecclesiasticae unitatis. *Accipimus* igitur *ipsi de suo quod ipse accepit de nostro*. In hoc enim sacramento accipimus de corpore et sanguine Christi, quae Filius Dei accepit de nostra natura. (*Opuscula Theologica*, 1:425)

Why does Thomas not simply cite the statement of faith, *Firmiter*, of Lateran IV when treating transubstantiation in *ST* III, q. 75? In light of his understanding of *sacra doctrina*, is this not exactly what we should expect? In order to understand why Thomas did not simply refer to the *Firmiter*, it is crucial to grasp that in his own doctrinal commentary on the decretal, Thomas understands the council to be expounding what the words of institution, according to Luke 22:19, entail—transubstantiation. For he understands any alternatives to transubstantiation to be excluded by the council's first affirmation, that of real presence. In short, according to Thomas, *Firmiter* does nothing but affirm the witness of sacred scripture and gesture in the direction to be taken by theology in light of unacceptable alternatives. Eucharistic real presence is based on sacred scripture, and transubstantiation is a necessary entailment. And this is exactly the route Thomas takes in his Eucharistic treatise in *ST* III. To put it differently, the fact that Thomas does not cite *Firmiter* in q. 75 of his Eucharistic treatise is a strong indication that he is intending to make the case for *Firmiter* by way of an extended exposition based on the same fundamental assertion, namely, that Christ's real presence is a revealed truth conveyed by the literal sense of sacred scripture (*ST* III, q. 75,

a. 1) and that this revealed truth calls for a metaphysical explication that issues necessarily in transubstantiation (a. 2). Making the case of *Firmiter* on the basis of the *intellectus fidei* with the help of sacred theology's privileged instrument—metaphysics—grants intelligibility to *Firmiter* and thereby prevents it from being misunderstood as merely a voluntarist act of magisterial authority. In short, my suggestion is that the reader of Thomas's Eucharistic treatise might, in light of Thomas's treatise, turn to Lateran IV's profession of faith and say: "I see."

APPENDIX 2

In the first question of the *Summa Theologiae*, Thomas unquestionably regards fidelity to God as the central requirement for those charged to expound *sacra doctrina*. We would, however, be profoundly mistaken if we were to infer from this that Thomas distinguishes between fidelity to God and obedience to the church's magisterium. Nevertheless, it is indeed the case that the fourteenth- and fifteenth-century conflicts between pope and councils eventually resulted in a form of papal primacy unknown to Thomas.[163] In light of these later developments, what Thomas does say about this matter is even more striking. For, arguably, he already held *in nuce* the truth that overcomes conciliarism, namely, a teaching magisterium with the pope at its head. Yves Congar, OP, brought together the most striking passages in Thomas's oeuvre that support and illustrate this claim:

Thus a Christian cannot be excused from the vice of error if he assents to the opinion of any teacher that is contrary to the manifest testimony of Scripture or is contrary to what is publicly held on the basis of the Church's authority (*Quodl.* III, 10).

If we consider Divine Providence which directs his Church by the Holy Spirit, so that it may not err, just as Jesus promised in Jn. 16:13 ... it is certain that for the judgment of the universal Church to err in matters of faith is an impossibility. Hence, we must stand by the decision of the Pope rather than the opinion of other men, even though they be learned in the

Scriptures. For the Pope has the right and duty to determine concerning the faith, a determination he indicates by his judgment (*Quodl.* IX, 16).

The custom of the Church has very great authority and ought always to be jealously observed in all things, since the very doctrine of Catholic doctors derives its authority from the Church. Thus, we ought to abide by the authority of the Church rather than that of Augustine or Jerome or of any other doctor (*Summa Theol.*, II-II, q. 10, a. 12).

Thus some doctors seem to have disagreed either with reference to matters that have no bearing on faith, whether they should be explained thus or so, or they disagreed regarding certain matters of faith which were not then determined by the Church. But, after their determination by the authority of the universal Church, if anyone should pertinaciously call such a decision into question, he would be considered a heretic. This authority resides principally in the Sovereign Pontiff. For we read in the Decretals (dist. XXIV, qu. 1, can. 12, Friedberg 970): "Whenever a question of faith is in dispute ..." (ibid., q. 11, a. 2, ad 3um).[164]

The best commentary on the profound correlation between fidelity to God and obedience to the church is to be found in Thomas's discussion of the object of faith in *ST* II-II, q. 1. Thomas moves from considering the contemplation of the first truth in the first article to considering "Whether it belongs to the Sovereign Pontiff to draw up a symbol of faith?" in the tenth article. Thomas suggests a profound interrelationship between the first and the tenth articles. In other words, fidelity to the first truth takes on concrete form in obedience to the church's teaching authority.

APPENDIX 3

Three essential points regarding Trent's decree need to be made briefly. First, the decree emphasizes "the conversion of the *whole* substance of the bread into the substance of the body of Christ our Lord, and of the *whole* substance of the wine into the substance of his blood" (emphasis added). In the background is an argument against the position of Durandus of St. Pourçain, OP (ca. 1275–1332), who understood Eucharistic conversion as a kind of transformation with an underlying subject implying a common matter between the

first and the second term of the conversion. As Stephen Brock rightly emphasizes, the Tridentine decree must be understood as a sound
rejection of Eucharistic conversion as a mere substantial transformation instead of a transubstantiation. The Tridentine emphasis on the
conversion of the whole substance of bread and the whole substance
of wine "would mean a substantial conversion that completely elim-
inates one substance, leaving a wholly distinct substance instead."[165]

Second, Engelbert Gutwenger, SJ, has convincingly argued in his
"Substanz und Akzidenz in der Eucharistielehre" that the Council of
Trent comprehensively endorsed the Eucharistic doctrine decreed
at the Council of Constance (1414–18). Especially with regard to
Eucharistic transubstantiation, the Fathers at Trent drew repeatedly
and thoroughly on the definitions and the entailed theological sup-
positions of Constance. The council Fathers at Constance, in turn,
unreservedly endorsed the metaphysical notions of substance and
accidents in relation to the Eucharist. Hence, it is very difficult, if
not impossible, to deny that the council Fathers at Trent not only ac-
knowledged the definitions of Constance as normative, but also the
underlying theological account, including the entailed metaphysical
principles.

The concrete issue at stake at Constance was the condemnation
of John Wycliffe's rejection of Eucharistic transubstantiation, spe-
cifically his teaching (with explicitly Scholastic concepts) that after
the consecration the bread was still bread, *verus panis*. Thus, if Gutwenger is correct that Trent, in essence, affirmed Constance, then it
is simply impossible to maintain (what has taken the form of popular lore in many circles) that Trent did not decree that transubstantiation is necessary for a correct *intellectus fidei*. Herbert McCabe, OP,
for example, states at the beginning of an otherwise intriguing med-
itation on "Eucharistic change": "The Council of Trent did not decree that Catholics should believe in transubstantiation: it just calls
it a most appropriate (*aptissime*) way of talking about the Eucharist,
presumably leaving it open whether there might not be other, per-
haps even more appropriate, ways of talking."[166]

Third, and closely related to the second point, one frequently en-
counters the claim that the Council of Trent used the word "species"
instead of "accident" in order to avoid any commitment to a "metaphysics of substance and accident." Gutwenger's extensive study
makes the convincing case that all the council Fathers, those favoring "species" as well as those favoring "accident," thought in broad-
ly Aristotelian terms.[167] Both "accident" and "species" belong to the
Aristotelian-Thomist conceptuality; they are largely used as syn-
onyms with "accident" emphasizing the order of being and referring
to the determination of substances, and "species" emphasizing the
order of knowledge and referring to the reception of things in the
mind by way of the species. "Accident" and "species" are aspects of
form. Even Edward Schillebeeckx, OP, agrees with Gutwenger on
this crucial point.[168] Schillebeeckx, however, disagrees vehement-
ly with Gutwenger's inference that the Council of Trent not only
used—inescapably in its conceptual context, Schillebeeckx would
say—but also *sanctioned* the descriptive use of the metaphysical
predicamentals "substance" and "accident" as the ineluctable ontological principles of the doctrine of faith in Eucharistic transubstantiation. It is important to clarify that sanctioning the Aristotelian categories is not the same as *imposing* them (or as some like to
put it, the Aristotelian "theory" of substance and accidents) as *de
fide*. Nor is it to say that these categories are the only way to unpack
"transubstantiation" theologically. In this regard, the matter clearly
comes down to the very nature of dogma and the nature of theology as an ecclesial discipline. If theology is understood as sacred theology or holy teaching (*sacra doctrina*) in the sense developed here,
Gutwenger's inference is legitimate and indeed makes good sense,
because metaphysics serves as a privileged instrument of sacred theology. If, however, theology is a contemporary hermeneutics of faith
and doctrine in light of an antecedent but constantly changing understanding of the human being—for example, as "modern man,"
"late-modern human," "postmodern de-centered subject," and soon
most likely postpostmodern "super-primate" (Daniel Dennett)—

Gutwenger's inference is incorrect. But if theology is an everchanging hermeneutics of faith, it is also unclear how any dogma can still be received and defended theologically *as* dogma, and this pertains to Nicaea and Chalcedon as well. Only one generation after Schillebeeckx, these inferences have already been drawn; and as the present "signs of the times" (*signa temporum*), the allegedly ineluctable contours of the "postmodern condition" have been invoked in order to understand the development of doctrine as the ongoing reconstruction of the faith itself.

APPENDIX 4

Let me at this point address a rather crude objection that most often occurs in the form of the question: must I believe in Aristotelian "substance metaphysics" in order to be able to believe in transubstantiation? In short, is Aristotelian "substance metaphysics" itself *de fide*?[169] Three things need to be said in response to this question, which in fact does not present a genuine objection but reflects rather a widespread misunderstanding.

First, faith is guided by the dominical words of consecration as interpreted by the church. And the church, from early on and in unbroken continuity, has understood them literally. Precisely this understanding has been reaffirmed every time it has been challenged by individual theologians such as Berengar, Wycliffe, and Zwingli. Hence, what is *de fide*, that is, what faith assents to, are the words "this is my body, this is my blood" in relationship to the bread and the wine understood as effectively signifying the complete conversion of what constitutes the bread and of the wine ("this" is bread, "this" is wine) into that which constitutes Christ's body and Christ's blood ("this" is Christ's body, "this" is Christ's blood). What is *de fide* is not the precise metaphysical description employed, but the "that" referred to by the words of consecration. And that "that" indeed has ineluctable ontological entailments. For the referent of the words of consecration is beheld by divine faith alone, and divine faith entails the assent of the intellect, which—crucially—is ordered to receive and understand in its first act being (*ens*) by way of substance. It is in this way that the notion of transubstantiation—which indeed is *de fide*—is called *aptissime* by Trent because it expresses the mystery of Christ's real, bodily presence in the Eucharistic elements.

Second, the *intellectus fidei*, accordingly, has to interpret and defend the proper assent of the intellect. In the course of this interpretation and defense, *sacra doctrina* draws upon that science that investigates the constitutive principles of being. Acknowledging that Aristotle has once and for all established this science of being, metaphysics—as Thomas does indeed acknowledge—does not entail an extrinsic, antecedent belief in metaphysics besides that of the student at the beginning of a course of studies. As Thomas observes: "The student must believe" (*Oportet addiscentem credere*).[170] This *credere* stands at the beginning of all learning, be it an art, a foreign language, or a science.

Third, it is very hard, if not impossible, for the *intellectus fidei* to interpret rightly and defend what is *de fide* about the Trinity and Christ's divinity and humanity without drawing upon the metaphysical notions and principles of essence, person, subsistence, nature, and relation. It is equally hard, if not impossible, to receive *de fide* the notion of "transubstantiation" as expressing the mystery of faith of Christ's real presence in the Eucharistic elements without the *intellectus fidei* drawing upon the metaphysical notions and principles of being, form and matter, substance, and accident. In this way the church's understanding of faith through dogma continues to direct the labors of sacred theology to its once privileged instrument, metaphysics as the science of being as being. This mode of inquiry is neither passé (for its proper formal object can never be passé) nor is it falsifiable on empirical grounds or on grounds of the mathematical natural sciences (for such a falsification could only occur by way of a superior science that does not exist, as metaphysics is, by definition of its subject matter, "first philosophy"). Accordingly, if one wants to be introduced into theological inquiry, one has to adopt the proper, natural faith of any student at the beginning of his or her course of studies. This means that for all contemporary students of theology, Aristotle's famous maxim—adopted by Thomas—holds regarding sacred theology as well as metaphysics: *Oportet addiscentem credere.* "The student must believe."

Endnotes

1. *Summa Theologiae* [hereafter "*ST*"] III, q. 65, a. 2: "Eucharistia ... ordinatur ad perfectionem finis." All English citations in this book from *ST* are taken from the translation of the Fathers of the English Dominican Province (New York: Benziger Bros., 1948). Alterations are indicated by brackets.

2. *ST* III, q. 76, a. 1: "Omnino necesse est confiteri secundum fidem Catholicam quod totus Christus sit in hoc sacramento."

3. For the theoretically most ambitious and arguably most influential account that rests its case on a quite uncritical adoption of Heidegger's critique of ontotheology and thereby weds itself too closely to the implications of an event-ontology profoundly at odds with the Christian Gospel, see Louis-Marie Chauvet, *Symbol and Sacrament: A Sacramental Reinterpretation of Christian Existence*, trans. Patrick Madigan, SJ, and Madeleine Beaumont (Collegeville, Minn.: Liturgical Press, 1995), 40–83. Chauvet's critique of Thomas's account of sacramental causality is driven by an unwarranted subscription to Martin Heidegger's critique of metaphysics. Following Heidegger, Cauvet's red herring is "ontotheology," the one unforgivable sin in Heidegger's taxonomy of philosophical faults. (See for a condensed and accessible version of Martin Heidegger's critique, "The Onto-theo-logical Constitution of Metaphysics," in *Identity and Difference*, trans. Joan Stambaugh [New York: Harper and Row, 1969], 42–74.) While it is still fashionable in uninformed circles to charge Thomas's metaphysics with the fault of "onto-theology," it has been shown incontrovertibly that this charge is misplaced by Thomist admirers and critics of Heidegger: see Gustav Siewert, *Das Schicksal der Metaphysik von Thomas zu Heidegger* (Freiburg: Johannes Verlag Einsiedeln, 2006 [1959]) and Yves Floucat, *Pour une métaphysique de l'être en son analogie: Heidegger et Thomas d'Aquin* (Paris: Artège Lethielleux,

2016). See also non-Thomist critics of Heidegger, such as David Bentley Hart, "The Offering of Names: Metaphysics, Nihilism, and Analogy," in his *The Hidden and the Manifest: Essays in Theology and Metaphysics* (Grand Rapids, Mich.: Eerdmans, 2017), 1–44, as well as John D. Caputo, *Heidegger and Aquinas: An Essay on Overcoming Metaphysics* (New York: Fordham University Press, 1982). See also the instructive special issue, edited by Serge-Thomas Bonino, OP, of *Revue Thomiste* 95, no. 1 (1995), and Hans Meyer, *Martin Heidegger und Thomas von Aquin* (Munich: Schöningh, 1964). It will probably take another generation of liturgical theologians to realize this insight and to correct the damage done by Chauvet's philosophical errancy. The real challenge is not, however, to deflect his charge of ontotheology against Thomas Aquinas but rather to answer the question to what degree his Heideggerian construal of ritual and symbol is actually compatible with the Catholic faith.

4. I gratefully borrow this felicitous rendition from John Betz, who used it to describe an earlier instantiation of "going upstream" in his penetrating review essay of *Reason and the Reasons of Faith*, ed. Paul J. Griffiths and Reinhard Hütter, *Pro Ecclesia* 16, no. 2 (2007): 218–30, at 222.

5. The widely influential Reformed theologian Jürgen Moltmann can stand as a paradigmatic voice for those who like to regard themselves as the ecumenical avant-garde. Here the axiom of the primacy and normativity of praxis, with theology as a subsequent after-the-fact reflection, finds an all-too-clear application in the mandate of the instantly norming praxis of intercommunion: "In eucharistic communion we actually do not arrive at a shared praxis on the basis of a shared theory. Rather, on the contrary, we arrive at a shared theory on the basis of a shared experience.... First comes the communion with Christ and then, after the eating and drinking, we may remain seated at his table and discuss our varying understandings of what has happened to us there." Jürgen Moltmann, "Ökumene im Zeitalter der Globalisierung. Die Enzyklika 'Ut Unum Sint' in evangelischer Sicht," in *Ökumene—wohin? Bischöfe und Theologen entwickeln Perspektiven*, ed. Bernd Jochen Hilberath and Jürgen Moltmann (Tübingen: Francke, 2000), 94 (author's translation). For a similar Catholic position, see Karl Rahner, *The Shape of the Church To Come*, trans. Edward Quinn (New York: Seabury, 1974), where he proposes that union of the churches be put prior to doctrinal agreement, and that the agreement be subsequently allowed to grow out of the preceding union.

6. See Alasdair MacIntyre, "The End of Education: The Fragmentation of the American University," *Commonweal* (October 20, 2006): 10–14.

7. Hence, natural theology (in the precise sense of the *praeambula fidei* as understood by Vatican I) is the primordial as well as indispensable conceptual

and ontological point of reference for its discursive and argumentative operation. In the *ordo disciplinae*, i.e., in the specific order of learning of sacred theology as a *scientia*, Thomas rightly advises that the training in the sciences that culminates in metaphysics antecedes the training in theology proper. Would that, in the deeply confused state of philosophical and theological studies, a glimpse of Aquinas's wisdom were to be caught and instantiated in an *ordo disciplinae* in which students would again move from A to B to C (an *ordo* that the natural sciences tellingly seem to have maintained).

8. The findings of the *intellectus fidei* depend, however, on the rectitude of judgment. Thomas argues that the rectitude of judgment comes about in two ways, first by a perfect use of reason and, second, by a certain connaturality with that which the judgment of reason is about. In matters divine, such connaturality comes about by the gift of the Spirit that is charity and that unites us with God. Consequently, this wisdom is caused, so to speak, by the will, that is, charity, while it subsists essentially in the intellect. Thomas states in *ST* II-II, q. 45, a. 2: "It belongs to the wisdom that is an intellectual virtue to pronounce right judgment about Divine things after reason has made its inquiry, but it belongs to wisdom as a gift of the Holy Spirit to judge aright about them on account of connaturality with them: thus Dionysius says (Div. Nom. ii) that 'Hierotheus is perfect in Divine things, for he not only learns, but is patient of, Divine things.' Now this sympathy or connaturality for Divine things is the result of charity, which unites us to God, according to 1 Cor. 6:17: 'He who is joined to the Lord, is one spirit.' Consequently wisdom which is a gift, has its cause in the will, which cause is charity, but it has its essence in the intellect, whose act is to judge aright." (Sic igitur circa res divinas ex rationis inquisitione rectum iudicium habere pertinet ad sapientiam quae est virtus intellectualis: sed rectum iudicium habet de eis secundum quandam connaturalitatem ad ipsa pertinet ad sapientiam secundum quod donum est Spiritus Sancti: sicut Dionysius dicit, in 2 cap. *De div. nom.*, quod Hierotheus est perfectus in divinis "non solum discens, sed et patiens divina." Huiusmodi autem compassio sive connaturalitas ad res divinas fit per caritatem, quae quidem unit nos Deo: secundum illud I ad Cor. 6, 17: "Qui adhaeret Deo unus spiritus est." Sic igitur sapientia quae est donum causam quidem habet in voluntate, scilicet caritatem: sed essentiam habet in intellectu, cuius actus est recte iudicare, ut supra habitum est.)

9. Johannes Feiner and Magnus Löhrer, eds., *Mysterium salutis: Grundriß heilsgeschichtlicher Dogmatik*, 5 vols. (Einsiedeln: Benziger, 1965–76).

10. On the central role of the economy of salvation and hence history and even narrative in the theological project of Thomas Aquinas, see Max Seckler, *Das Heil in der Geschichte: Geschichtstheologisches Denken bei Thomas von Aquin*

(Munich: Kösel, 1964), and Thomas S. Hibbs, *Dialectic and Narrative in Aquinas: An Interpretation of the* Summa contra gentiles (Notre Dame, Ind.: University of Notre Dame Press, 1995).

11. For the classical argument promoting this lore, it is still instructive to read the *spiritus rector* of early twentieth-century liberal Protestantism, Adolf von Harnack's *What Is Christianity?*, trans. Thomas Bailey Saunders (New York: Putnam, 1901), and especially his *Lehrbuch der Dogmengeschichte*, 3 vols. (Freiburg: Mohr, 1887–90). For the perpetuation of this prejudice into the Luther-renaissance of the early twentieth century, see Wilhelm Link, *Das Ringen Luthers um die Freiheit der Theologie von der Philosophie*, 2nd ed. (Munich: Kaiser, 1955). The most serious philosophical barrier in the twentieth century against returning to those profound Christian sources who freely drew upon metaphysics is Martin Heidegger's sprawling *oeuvre*. It is arguably due to his influence that most post-conciliar theologians still take it as a simple given that "metaphysics" must be—what else could it be!—a closed system of thinking allegedly governed by what remains unthought and thereby inflicting fatal closure on thought. Of course, thus conceived, metaphysics is nothing but a mental cage from which one must escape in order to be able again to "think"—theologically. To put it mildly, Thomas would have been surprised to learn about his captivity, as would have, I dare to venture, Aristotle.

12. John Paul II, *Fides et Ratio*, Encyclical Letter, September 14, 1998, par. 83.

13. For a profound and lucid treatment of substance in dialogue with modern science and thought, see the paper by one of the best Thomist metaphysicians of the twentieth century, Lawrence Dewan, OP, "The Importance of Substance," in his *Form and Being: Studies in Thomistic Metaphysics* (Washington, D.C.: The Catholic University of America Press, 2006), 96–130.

14. As its privileged instrument, metaphysics plays an indispensable role in sacred theology. For sacred theology to ignore God as the transcendent cause of the effects of nature not only means to forgo the insights attainable from a metaphysical inquiry that ascends from finite to infinite being but also to commit the claim to transcendence entailed in a divine revelation that is historical and definitive to the enclosure of the immanent frame (Charles Taylor) and hence to unintelligibility. Rudi te Velde puts the matter succinctly: "Without reason's *manuductio* [act of guiding], by which the subject of the revealed doctrine of faith is given an intelligible determination, the Christian *revelatio* cannot be understood to be what it is assumed to be: knowledge which is true of God. Without the *manuductio* of metaphysics, leading to a transcendent reality, the Christian revelation will lapse into the immanence of human history, at least in the sense that its putative reference to transcendence remains unintelli-

gible." Rudi te Velde, *Aquinas on God: The 'Divine Science' of the* Summa Theologiae (Burlington, Vt.: Ashgate, 2006), 30. According to Aquinas, a theology that eschews the assistance of metaphysics will most likely fall short in achieving the *intellectus fidei*, the maximum of intelligibility and communicability of the revealed knowledge of God and God's saving work this side of the beatific vision.

15. In the wake of rationalism, a significant strand of modern theology tends to reduce genuine supernatural mysteries—the Trinity, creation *ex nihilo*, original sin, the incarnation, the theandric nature of Christ, Eucharistic conversion, predestination, and eschatology—into conceptual problems or puzzles that call for a conceptual resolution. Drawing upon Gabriel Marcel and Jacques Maritain, Thomas G. Weinandy defends the genuine nature of mystery against the usurpations of rationalism in theology: "Maritain states that where there is mystery 'the intellect has to penetrate more and more deeply the *same* object.' The mystery, by the necessity of its subject matter, remains.... Many theologians today, having embraced the Enlightenment presupposition and the scientific method that it fostered, approach theological issues as if they were scientific problems to be solved rather than mysteries to be discerned and clarified. However, the true goal of theological inquiry is not the resolution of theological *problems*, but the discernment of what the *mystery* of faith is." Thomas G. Weinandy, OFM Cap., *Does God Suffer?* (Notre Dame, Ind.: University of Notre Dame Press, 2000), 31–32. Weinandy articulates here a theological insight that was advanced in great depth and sophistication in the second half of the nineteenth century by Matthias Joseph Scheeben in his *Mysteries of Christianity*, trans. Cyril Vollert, SJ (St. Louis, Mo.: Herder, 1951), and in the first half of the twentieth century by Réginald Garrigou-Lagrange, OP, in his *The Sense of Mystery: Clarity and Obscurity in the Intellectual Life*, trans. Matthew K. Minerd (Steubenville, Ohio: Emmaus Academic, 2017).

16. It is "metaphysics" conceived along the lines of Hegel's rigorous explanatory conceptualism of "metaphysics as science in the strictest and most complete sense" that Wittgenstein abhorred in his *Blue Book*—see *The Blue and Brown Books* (Oxford: Blackwell, 1958), 18—and over against which he claimed that "philosophy really *is* 'purely descriptive.'" *Wittgenstein and the Vienna Circle: Conversations Recorded by Friedrich Waismann*, ed. Brian McGuinness (Oxford: Blackwell, 1979), 117. I entertain strong and warrantable doubts that any but the most degenerate versions (and those tend to be of hearsay only) of Aristotelian natural philosophy and metaphysics could fall under Wittgenstein's verdict.

17. Here is St. Luke's version of the *paradosis* of Christ's words at the Last Supper: "τοῦτό ἐστιν τὸ σῶμά μου τὸ ὑπὲρ ὑμῶν διδόμενον."

CHAPTER 1

18. *ST* I, q. 1, a. 1: "Necessarium fuit ad humanam salutem, esse doctrinam quandam secundum revelationem divinam, praeter philosophicas disciplinas, quae ratione humana investigantur. Primo quidem, quia homo ordinatur ad Deum sicut at quendam finem qui comprehensionem rationis excedit.... Finem autem oportet esse praecognitum hominibus, qui suas intentiones et actiones debent ordinare in finem. Unde necessarium fuit homini ad salutem, quod ei nota fierent quaedam per revelationem divinam, quae rationem humanam excedunt. Ad ea etiam quae de Deo ratione humana investigari possunt, necessarium fuit hominem instrui revelatione divina. Quia veritas de Deo, per rationem investigata, a paucis, et per longum tempus, et cum admixtione multorum errorum, homini proveniret; a cuius tamen veritatis cognitione dependet tota hominis salus, quae in Deo est. Ut igitur salus hominibus et convenientius et certius proveniat, necessarium fuit quod de divinis per divinam revelationem instruantur."

19. When we compare Thomas's discussion of this topic in the *Summa* with his early treatment of it in his commentary on Lombard's *Sentences* (see *Scriptum super libros Sententiarum magistri Petri Lombardi episcopi Parisiensis* [hereafter "*Sent.*"] IV, d. 8, q. 1, a. 1), we realize that Thomas intentionally inserted this article right at the beginning of his discussion of sacramental conversion. While in his *Sentences* commentary (which are based on his lectures on the work), Thomas was expected to remain faithful to the outline and questions given by Peter Lombard and discussed by his predecessors, especially Bonaventure, in the *Summa Theologiae* Thomas develops a new scheme with a new outline and format that offers him the freedom to address new and different questions.

20. *ST* III, q. 75, a. 1. In another way, this article can be read as a highly condensed reception of the early medieval and pre-Scholastic Eucharistic doctrine. For a still greatly informative study of this rich period of pre-Scholastic theological contemplation of the mystery, see Josef Geiselmann, *Die Eucharistielehre der Vorscholastiker* (Paderborn: Schöningh, 1926).

21. *ST* III, q. 75, a. 1, co.: "Ideo oportuit ut aliquid plus haberet sacrificium novae legis a Christo institutum: ut scilicet contineret ipsum passum non solum in significatione vel figura, sed etiam in rei veritate. Et ideo hoc sacramentum, quod ipsum Christum realiter continet, ut Dionysius dicit, 3 cap. *Eccles. Hierar., est perfectivum omnium sacramentorum aliorum*, in quibus virtus Christi participatur."

22. Ibid.: "Interim tamen nec sua praesentia corporali in hac peregrinatione destituit, sed per veritatem corporis et sanguinis sui nos sibi coniungit in hoc

sacramento. Unde ipse dicit, *Ioan. 6*, [57]: *Qui manducat meam carnem et bibit meum sanguinem, in me manet et ego in eo.* Unde hoc sacramentum est maximae caritatis signum, et nostrae spei sublevamentum, ex tam familiari coniunctione Christi ad nos."

23. Ibid.: "Et quia fides est invisibilium, sicut divinitatem suam nobis exhibet Christus invisibiliter, ita et in hoc sacramento carnem suam nobis exhibet invisibili modo."

24. Ibid.: "Verum corpus Christi et sanguinem esse in hoc sacramento, non sensu deprehendi potest, sed sola fide, quae auctoritati divinae innititur. Unde super illud Luc. 22, [19], 'Hoc est corpus meum quod pro vobis tradetur,' dicit Cyrillus: 'Non dubites an hoc verum sit, sed potius suscipe verba Salvatoris in fide: cum enim sit veritas, non mentitur.'"

25. *Patrologia Graeca*, ed. J.-P. Migne (Paris, 1857–66), 72:92.

26. At this point it is appropriate to call to mind the status and role of the doctors of the church in Thomas's hierarchy of authorities. According to *ST* I, q. 1, a. 8, ad 2, the doctors cited have an authority intrinsic to *sacra doctrina*, albeit only a probable one. That is, church doctors and their writings do have a clearly lesser authority than statements of faith produced by church councils and ratified by the pope. Only the latter have an authority for *sacra doctrina* that is intrinsic as well as certain.

27. *ST* I, q. 1, a. 2: "Et hoc modo sacra doctrina est scientia, quia procedit ex principiis notis lumine superioris scientiae, quae scilicet est scientia Dei et beatorum. Unde sicut musica credit principia tradita sibi ab arithmetico, ita doctrina sacra credit principia revelata sibi a Deo."

28. *ST* I, q. 1, a. 10, co.: "Auctor sacrae Scripturae est Deus."

29. *ST* II-II, q. 5, a. 3, ad 2: "Omnibus articulis fidei inhaeret fides propter unum medium, scilicet propter veritatem primam propositam nobis in Scripturis secundum doctrinam Ecclesiae intellectis sane."

30. *ST* III q. 75, a. 1, s.c.: "Hilary says (*De Trin.*, viii [PL 10:247]): 'There is no room for doubt regarding the truth of Christ's body and blood; for now by our Lord's own declaring and by our faith His flesh is truly food, and His blood is truly drink.' And Ambrose says (*De Sacram.*, vi [cap. 1; PL 16:473]): 'As the Lord Jesus Christ is God's true Son, so is it Christ's true flesh which we take, and His true blood which we drink.'" *PL = Patrologia Latina*, ed. J.-P. Migne (Paris, 1844–55).

31. For *doctrina* not as a "thing" but an act; see Frederick Christian Bauerschmidt, "That the Faithful Become the Temple of God," in *Reading John with St. Thomas Aquinas: Theological Exegesis and Speculative Theology*, ed. Michael Dauphinais and Matthew Levering (Washington, D.C.: The Catholic University of America Press, 2005), 293–311.

32. Ludwig Wittgenstein, *Philosophische Untersuchungen* §129, in *Schriften* (Frankfurt: Suhrkamp, 1960), 346: "Man kann es nicht bemerken,—weil man es immer vor Augen hat."

33. Erik Peterson, "Theologie als Wissenschaft," in his *Theologie als Wissenschaft: Aufsätze und Thesen*, ed. Gerhard Sauter (Munich: Kaiser, 1971), 150; the translation is taken from the discussion of Peterson in my *Suffering Divine Things: Theology as Church Practice*, trans. Doug Stott (Grand Rapids, Mich.: Eerdmans, 1999), 96–102 and 230–33 at 232. More recently, Peterson's important essay has been made available in a new edition of his works: Erik Peterson, *Ausgewählte Schriften*, vol. 1: *Theologische Traktate* (Würzburg: Echter, 1994), 3–22. See now the English translation: *Theological Tractates*, ed. and trans. Michael J. Hollerich (Stanford, Calif.: Stanford University Press, 2011).

34. Peterson, "Theologie als Wissenschaft," 149, from Hütter, *Suffering*, 231.

35. See Barbara Nichtweiss, *Erik Peterson: Neue Sicht auf Leben und Werk* (Freiburg: Herder, 1992), 384; and regarding the relationship between Peterson and Barth while both were lecturers at the University of Göttingen, see 505–12; and on the dispute over the treatise "What Is Theology?," see 512–17. According to Nichtweiss, Karl Barth regularly attended Peterson's lecture course on Thomas Aquinas, which, in all likelihood, was Barth's first real encounter with the theology of Aquinas.

36. *ST* II-II, q. 5, a. 3, co.: "Formale autem obiectum fidei est veritas prima secundum quod manifestatur in Scripturis sacris et doctrinae Ecclesiae." The Editio Piana (Rome, 1570) contains the following addition, absent from the Editio Leonina (Rome, 1882–): "quae procedit ex veritate prima."

37. It was through the initiative of St. Julienne of Mont-Cornillon that this feast began to be celebrated around 1240.

38. See Jean-Pierre Torrell, *Saint Thomas Aquinas*, vol. 1: *The Person and His Work*, trans. Robert Royal (Washington, D.C.: The Catholic University of America Press, 1996), 129–36.

39. *The Aquinas Prayer Book: The Prayers and Hymns of St. Thomas Aquinas*, ed. and trans. Robert Anderson and Johann Moser (Manchester, N.H.: Sophia Institute Press, 2000), 102–4. For a profound theological interpretation of Thomas's hymn *Lauda Sion Salvatorem* (composed for the new feast of Corpus Christi) as a surpassing poetic articulation of the mystery of Christ's real presence in the Eucharist—completely consonant with his account of transubstantiation but expressing in a nondiscursive doxological way the profoundly personal and relational character of the mystery—see Jan-Heiner Tück, *A Gift of Presence: The Theology and Poetry of the Eucharist in Thomas Aquinas*, trans. Scott G. Hefelfinger (Washington, D.C.: The Catholic University of America Press, 2018), 209–28.

CHAPTER 2

40. First Vatican Council, *Dogmatic Constitution on the Catholic Faith, Dei Filius*, April 24, 1870, c. 4.

41. Cf. Council of Trent, *Decree on the Holy Eucharist*, c. 3.

42. Pope Pius XII, *Humani Generis*, Encyclical Letter, in *AAS* 42 (1950): 578.

43. Cyrille de Jérusalem, *Catéchèses mystagogiques*, ed. Piedagnel and P. Paris, Sources Chrétiennes 126 (Paris: Cerf, 1966), 138.

44. *Catechism of the Catholic Church*, §1374: "In the most blessed sacrament of the Eucharist 'the body and blood, together with the soul and divinity, of our Lord Jesus Christ and, therefore, *the whole Christ is truly, really, and substantially contained*' [Council of Trent (1551): Denzinger 1651]." See also §1376: "The Council of Trent summarizes the Catholic faith by declaring: 'Because Christ our Redeemer said that it was truly his body that he was offering under the species of bread, it has always been the conviction of the Church of God, and this holy Council now declares again, that by the consecration of the bread and wine there takes place a change of the whole substance of the bread into the substance of the body of Christ our Lord and of the whole substance of the wine into the substance of his blood. This change the holy Catholic Church has fittingly and properly called transubstantiation' [Council of Trent (1551): Denzinger 1642; cf. Mt 26:26; Mk 14:22; Lk 22:19; 1 Cor 11:24]."

45. Joseph Ratzinger, "Das Problem der Transsubstantiation und die Frage nach dem Sinn der Eucharistie," *Theologische Quartalschrift* 147 (1967): 129–59.

46. Here I draw upon, and agree with, Horst Seidl, "Zum Substanzbegriff der katholischen Transsubstantiationslehre: Erkenntnistheoretische und metaphysische Erörterungen," *Forum Katholische Theologie* 11 (1995): 1–16.

47. Joseph Ratzinger provides an excellent example of such a hermeneutical approximation in his above-mentioned 1967 essay "Das Problem der Transsubstantiation und die Frage nach dem Sinn der Eucharistie." As Pope Benedict XVI, he continues such hermeneutical approximation in his post-synodal apostolic exhortation *Sacramentum Caritatis* (2007), where he seems to be at pains to use traditional terminology that at the same time does not commit him to one particular school of thought (e.g., "quorum sub specie" in par. 8, and "substantialis transmutatio" in par. 11): "The substantial conversion [*substantialis transmutatio*] of bread and wine into his body and blood introduces within creation the principle of a radical change [*principium extremae mutationis*], a sort of 'nuclear fission,' to use an image familiar to us today, which penetrates to the heart of all being, a change meant to set off a process which transforms reality, a process leading ultimately to the transfiguration of the entire world, to the point where God will be all in all (cf. 1 Cor 15:28)" (par. 11). Such a procedure,

however, is categorically different from slicing dogma itself into two parts, so to speak, a transcendent "intention" that affirms the truth of faith on the one side, and on the other side, a time-conditioned, conceptual way of "expressing" said intention, this second part being in continuous need of contextual updating by replacing purportedly outdated conceptual tools with contemporary ones.

CHAPTER 3

48. Edward Schillebeeckx, OP, *The Eucharist*, trans. N. D. Smith (New York: Sheed and Ward, 1968), 94.

49. For an astute account of what is at stake in the conflict between a philosophical affirmation and a philosophical negation of substance, see Henry Babcock Veatch, *Two Logics: The Conflict between Classical and Neo-Analytic Philosophy* (Evanston, Ill.: Northwestern University Press, 1969), and for a position that argues for the compatibility of quantum mechanics with hylomorphism, and therefore with the notions of substantial form and substance, see William A. Wallace, OP, "Thomism and Modern Science," *The Thomist* 32 (1968): 67–83.

50. Jacques Maritain, "La philosophie et l'unité des sciences," in his *Quatre essais sur l'esprit dans sa condition charnelle* (Paris: Alsatia, 1956), 253–54; translation from Charles Cardinal Journet, *The Mass: The Presence of the Sacrifice of the Cross*, trans. Victor Szczureck, O. Praem. (South Bend, Ind.: St. Augustine's Press, 2008), 157.

51. Council of Trent, thirteenth session (October 11, 1551), chap. 4, "De transsubstantiatione," in *Decrees of the Ecumenical Councils*, vol. 2: *Trent—Vatican II*, ed. Norman P. Tanner, SJ (Washington, D.C.: Georgetown University Press, 1990), 695. Heinrich Denzinger, *Enchiridion symbolorum definitionum et declarationum de rebus fidei et morum: Kompendium der Glaubensbekenntnisse und kirchlichen Lehrentscheidungen, Lateinisch-Deutsch*, ed. Peter Hünermann, 40th ed. (Freiburg: Herder, 2005) [hereafter "Denzinger"], no. 1642: "Per consecrationem panis et vini conversionem fieri totius substantiae panis in substantiam corporis Christi Domini nostri, et totius substantiae vini in substantiam sanguinis eius. Quae conversio convenienter et proprie a sancta catholica Ecclesia transsubstantiatio est appellata." All citations from the Second Vatican Council and the Council of Trent are taken from Tanner.

52. John Paul II, *Fides et Ratio*, par. 66.

53. Ralph McInerny, *Praeambula Fidei: Thomism and the God of the Philosophers* (Washington, D.C.: The Catholic University of America Press, 2006), 175n6.

54. In its document "On the Interpretation of Dogmas," the International Theological Commission reminds us unequivocally that this very procedure

is indeed of an enduring importance for the interpretation of the mysteries of faith: "It was already the First Vatican Council which taught that a deeper insight into the mysteries of faith may be possible in considering them by way of analogy with natural knowledge and relating them to the ultimate goal of human beings (DS 3016)." *Origins* 20, no. 1 (May 17, 1990): 13.

55. Lawrence Dewan, OP, "The Importance of Substance," in *Form and Being*, 110. Thomas discusses the primacy of substance among beings in *In duodecim libros Metaphysicorum Aristotelis expositio* [hereafter "*In Meta.*"] VII, l. 1 (Marietti, nos. 1246–59). See also his discussion of what Dewan felicitously calls "the causal 'flow' of all beings from substances" (110) in *ST* I, q. 77, a. 6: "The substantial and the accidental form partly agree and partly differ. They agree in this, that each is an act [*actus*]; and that by each of them something is after a manner actual [*quodammodo in actu*]. They differ, however, in two respects. First, because the substantial form makes a thing to exist absolutely [*facit esse simpliciter*], and its subject is something purely potential. But the accidental form does not make a thing to exist absolutely but to be such, or so great, or in some particular condition [*esse tale, aut tantum, aut aliquo modo se habens*]; for its subject is an actual being. Hence it is clear that actuality is observed in the substantial form prior to its being observed in the subject: and since that which is first in a genus is the cause in that genus, the substantial form causes existence in its subject [*forma substantialis causat esse in actu in suo subiecto*]. On the other hand, actuality is observed in the subject of the accidental form prior to its being observed in the accidental form; wherefore the actuality of the accidental form is caused by the actuality of the subject. So the subject, forasmuch as it is in potentiality, is receptive of the accidental form: but forasmuch as it is in act, it produces it. This I say of the proper and 'per se' accident; for with regard to the extraneous accident, the subject is receptive only, the accident being caused by an extrinsic agent. Secondly, substantial and accidental forms differ, because, since that which is the less principal exists for the sake of that which is the more principal, matter therefore exists on account of the substantial form; while on the contrary, the accidental form exists on account of the completeness of the subject."

56. Dewan, "The Importance of Substance," 110.

57. John F. Wippel, *The Metaphysical Thought of Thomas Aquinas: From Finite Being to Uncreated Being* (Washington, D.C.: The Catholic University of America Press, 2000), 216.

58. Ibid., 211.

59. "The mode or way in which words signify does not immediately follow upon the mode of being of such things, but only as mediated by the way in which such things are understood. To put this another way, words are like-

nesses or signs of thoughts, and thoughts themselves are likenesses of things, as Thomas recalls from Bk I of Aristotle's *De interpretatione*" (ibid.). That is, "Thomas follows Aristotle in singling out being as it exists outside the mind and is divided into the ten predicaments.... [Therefore,] in whatever ways being is predicated, in so many ways is *esse* signified, that is, in so many ways is something signified to be" (ibid., 212). For an excellent analysis of this complex matter, see also John P. O'Callaghan, *Thomist Realism and the Linguistic Turn: Toward a More Perfect Form of Existence* (Notre Dame, Ind.: University of Notre Dame Press, 2003).

60. *In octo libros Physicorum Aristotelis expositio* [hereafter "*In Phys.*"] III, l. 5 (Marietti, no. 322); translation from Thomas Aquinas, *Commentary on Aristotle's Physics*, trans. Richard J. Blackwell, Richard J. Spath, and W. Edmund Thirlkel (Notre Dame, Ind.: Dumb Ox Books, 1999), 160 (no. 322). "Ad horum igitur evidentiam sciendum est quod ens dividitur in decem praedicamenta non univoce, sicut genus in species, sed secundum diversum modum essendi. Modi autem essendi proportionales sunt modis praedicandi. Praedicando enim aliquid de aliquo altero, dicimus hoc esse illud: unde et decem genera entis dicuntur decem praedicamenta. Tripliciter autem fit omnis praedicatio. Unus quidem modus est, quando de aliquo subiecto praedicatur id quod pertinet ad essentiam eius, ut cum dico *Socrates est homo, vel homo est animal*; et secundum hoc accipitur praedicamentum *substantiae*." *In Phys.* III, l. 5 (Marietti, no. 322).

61. See Aristotle, *Categories*, chaps. 4 and 5.

62. *ST* I, q. 3, a. 5, ad 1: "The word substance signifies not only what exists of itself [*quod est per se esse*]—for existence [*esse*] cannot of itself be a genus ... [substance] also signifies an essence [*essentia*] that has the property of existing in this way—namely, of existing of itself; this existence [*esse*], however, is not its essence [*essentia*]." (Substantiae nomen non significat hoc solum quod est per se esse, quia hoc quod est esse, non potest per se esse genus.... Sed significat essentiam cui competit sic esse, idest per se esse, quod tamen esse non est ipsa eius essentia.)

63. *De potentia Dei*, q. 7, a. 3, ad 4: "According to Avicenna (*Metaph.* iii, 8) substance is not rightly defined as a self-subsistent being: for *being* cannot be the genus of a thing according to the Philosopher (*Metaph.* ii, 3), because nothing can be added to being that has not a share of being, and a difference should not be a part of the genus. If, however, substance can be defined notwithstanding that it is the most universal of genera, its definition will be a *thing whose quiddity is competent to have being not in a subject*. Hence the definition of substance cannot be applied to God, whose quiddity is not distinct from his being. Wherefore God is not contained in the genus of substance but is above all substance." (Ens

per se non est definitio substantiae, ut Avicenna dicit. Ens enim non potest esse alicuius genus, ut probat philosophus, cum nihil possit addi ad ens quod non participet ipsum; differentia vero non debet participare genus. Sed si substantia possit habere definitionem, non obstante quod est genus generalissimum, erit eius definitio: *quod substantia est res cuius quidditati debetur esse non in aliquo.* Et sic non conveniet definitio substantiae Deo, qui non habet quidditatem suam praeter suum esse. Unde Deus non est in genere substantiae, sed est supra omnem substantiam.)

64. See *In librum beati Dionysii de divinis nominibus expositio,* c. 5, l. 2 (Marietti, no. 660): "Ipsum esse creatum est quaedam participatio Dei et similitudo ipsius." See also *Sent.* I, q. 8, a. 1, q.c. 1, ad 2, and a. 12; *De Veritate,* q. 21, a. 2, ad 2, and q. 22, a. 2, ad 2; *SCG* III.66.

65. *SCG* I.43.8: "Considered absolutely, being is infinite, since there are infinite and infinite modes in which it can be participated. If, then, the being of some thing is finite, that being must be limited by something other that is somehow its cause." (Ipsum esse absolute consideratum infinitum est: nam ab infinitis et infinitis modis participari possibile est. Si igitur alicuius esse sit finitum, oportet quod limitetur esse illud per aliquid aliud quod sit aliqualiter causa illius esse.)

66. *ST* I, q. 45, a. 4: "To be created is, in a manner, to be made, as was shown above [*ST* I, q. 44, a. 2, ad 2 and 3]. Now, to be made is directed to the being of a thing [*Fieri autem ordinatur ad esse rei*]. Hence to be made and to be created properly belong to whatever being belongs; which, indeed, belongs properly to subsisting things, whether they are simple things, as in the case of separate substances, or composite, as in the case of material substances. For being belongs to that which has being—that is, to what subsists in its own being [*Illi enim proprie convenit esse, quod habet esse; et hoc est subsistens in suo esse*]. But forms and accidents and the like are called beings, not as if they themselves were, but because something is by them; as whiteness is called a being, inasmuch as its subject is white by it. Hence, according to the Philosopher (Metaph. vii, text 2) accident is more properly said to be 'of a being' than 'a being' [*magis proprie dicitur entis quam ens*]. Therefore, as accidents and forms and the like non-subsisting things are to be said to co-exist rather than to exist, so they ought to be called rather 'concreated' than 'created' things; whereas, properly speaking, created things are subsisting beings [*subsistentia*]."

67. See *De principiis naturae* 1, 6; *In Aristotelis librum de anima commentarium* [hereafter "*In de An.*"] II, l. 1 (Marietti, no. 218), and l. 2 (Marietti, nos. 235–37); *In Phys.* I, l. 2 (Marietti, no. 14) and l. 12 (Marietti, no. 108), and II, l. 2 (Marietti, no. 149); *In Meta.* VII, l. 17 (Marietti, no. 1680); *ST* III, q. 2, a. 1.

68. *ST* III, q. 75, a. 6, obj. 1: "Videtur quod, facta consecratione, remaneat in hoc sacramento forma substantialis panis. Dictum est enim quod, facta consecratione, remaneant accidentia. Sed, cum panis sit quiddam artificiale, etiam forma eius est accidens. Ergo remanet, facta consecratione."

69. *ST* III, q. 75, a. 6, ad 1: "Nihil prohibet arte fieri aliquid cuius forma non est accidens, sed forma substantialis, sicut arte possunt produci ranae et serpentes. Talem enim formam non producit ars virtute propria, sed virtute naturalium principiorum. Et hoc modo producit formam substantialem panis, virtute ignis decoquentis materiam ex farina et aqua confectam."

70. See the commentary by Damasus Winzen, OSB, in Thomas von Aquin, *Summa Theologica*, Deutsch-Lateinische Ausgabe (Die Deutsche Thomas-Ausgabe), vol. 30: *Das Geheimnis der Eucharistie* (Salzburg: Verlag Anton Pustet, 1938), 414.

71. Christopher M. Brown, "Artifacts, Substances, and Transubstantiation: Solving a Puzzle for Aquinas's Views," *The Thomist* 71, no. 1 (2007): 89–112, at 112.

72. Ibid.

73. Ibid.

74. As cultural products, bread and wine acquire important symbolic significations. This is so in many cultures and especially in the unfolding encounter of the triune God with the people of Israel narrated in scripture. This symbolic signification is assumed, elevated, and perfected by Christ in the institution of the Eucharist at the Last Supper and is therefore crucial for understanding the *sacramental* nature of the Eucharist, a topic touched upon later. Yet the historical fact that bread and wine are cultural products and thereby inherently open to carrying profound symbolic signification is irrelevant in regard to the metaphysical consideration as to whether bread and wine are substances.

75. Aquinas, *Commentary on Aristotle's* Physics, 160. *In Phys.* III, l. 5 (Marietti, no. 322): "Alius autem modus est quo praedicatur de aliquo id quod non est de essentia eius, tamen inhaeret ei. Quod quidem vel se habet ex parte materiae subiecti, et secundum hoc est praedicamentum *quantitatis* (nam quantitas proprie consequitur materiam ...); aut consequitur formam, et sic est praedicamentum *qualitatis.*"

76. *ST* III, q. 77, a. 2: "The first disposition of matter is dimensive quantity, hence Plato also assigned 'great' and 'small' as the first differences of matter (Aristotle, *Metaph.* iv). And because the first subject is matter, the consequence is that all other accidents are related to their subject through the medium of dimensive quantity; just as the first subject of color is said to be the surface, on which account some have maintained that dimensions are the substances of bodies, as is said in *Metaph.* iii." (Quia primum subiectum est materia, conse-

quens est quod omnia alia accidentia referantur ad subiectum mediante quantitate dimensiva, sicut et primum subiectum coloris dicitur superficies esse, ratione cuius quidam posuerunt dimensiones esse substantias corporum, ut dicitur
in III *Metaphys.*)

77. In *Metaph.* V, l. 15 (Marietti, no. 977): "Quantum dicitur quod est divisibile in ea quae insunt." For a lucid exposition, see Leo J. Elders, SVD, *Die Naturphilosophie des Thomas von Aquin* (Weilheim-Bierbronnen: Gustav-Siewerth-
Akademie, 2004), 70. For the precise differentiation between proper quantitative divisibility and other kinds of divisibilities, see John of St. Thomas, *Cursus
philosophicus Thomisticus* I, Log., part II, q. XVI, a. 1 (463).

78. Elders, *Die Naturphilosophie des Thomas von Aquin*, 75. He is drawing his
image from John of St. Thomas, *Cursus Philosophicus Thomisticus* I, Log., part II,
q. XVI, a. 1 (466): "In sententia S. Thomae propria et formalis ratio quantitatis
est extensio partium in ordine ad totum, quod est reddere partes formaliter integrantes. Unde remota quantitate, substantia non habet partes integrales formaliter in ratione partis ordinatas et distinctas."

79. John of St. Thomas, *Cursus Philosophicus Thomisticus* I, Log., part II,
q. XVI, a. 1 (464): "Quantitas dicitur praebere partes integrales substantiae, non
constituendo illas, sed ordinando inter se. Et haec ordinatio accidentalis est."

80. *ST* III, q. 77, a. 2: "It must be maintained that the principle of individuation is dimensive quantity. For that something is naturally in another one
solely, is due to the fact that that other is undivided in itself, and distinct from
all others. But it is on account of quantity that substance can be divided, as is
said in *Phys.* i. And therefore dimensive quantity itself is a particular principle
of individuation in forms of this kind, namely, inasmuch as forms numerically
distinct are in different parts of the matter. Hence also dimensive quantity has
of itself a kind of individuation, so that we can imagine several lines of the same
species, differing in position, which is included in the notion of this quantity;
for it belongs to dimension for it to be "'quantity having position'" (Aristotle,
Categor. iv), and therefore dimensive quantity can be the subject of the other
accidents, rather than the other way about." (Individuationis principium est
quantitas dimensiva. Ex hoc enim aliquid est natum esse in uno solo, quod illud
est in se indivisum et divisum ab omnibus aliis. Divisio autem accidit substantiae ratione quantitatis, ut dicitur in I *Physic.* Et ideo ipsa quantitas dimensiva
est quoddam individuationis principium huiusmodi formis, inquantum scilicet
diversae formae numero sunt in diversis partibus materiae. Unde ipsa quantitas
dimensiva secundum se habet quandam individuationem, ita quod possumus
imaginari plures lineas eiusdem speciei differentes positione, quae cadit in ratione quantitatis huius; convenit enim dimensioni quod sit *quantitas positionem*

habens. Et ideo potius quantitas dimensiva potest esse subiectum aliorum accidentium quam e converso.)

81. Joseph Bobik, "Dimensions of the Individuation of Bodily Substances," *Philosophical Studies* 4 (1954): 62.

82. Charles Cardinal Journet, *The Mass: The Presenence of the Sacrifice of the Cross*, trans. Victor Szczurek, O. Praem. (South Bend, Ind.: St. Augustine's Press, 2008), 153.

83. *ST* III, q. 76, a. 1: "Omnino necesse est confiteri secundum fidem Catholicam quod totus Christus sit in hoc sacramento. Sciendum tamen quod aliquid Christi est in hoc sacramento dupliciter: uno modo, quasi ex vi sacramenti; alio modo, ex naturali concomitantia. Ex vi quidem sacramenti, est sub speciebus huius sacramenti id in quod directe convertitur substantia panis et vini praeexistens, prout significatur per verba formae, quae sunt effectiva in hoc sacramento sicut et in ceteris: puta cum dicitur, *Hoc est corpus meum. Hic est sanguis meus.* Ex naturali autem concomitantia est in hoc sacramento illud quod realiter est coniunctum ei in quod praedicta conversio terminatur. Si enim aliqua duo sunt realiter coniuncta, ubicumque est unum realiter, oportet et aliud esse: sola enim operatione animae discernuntur quae realiter sunt coniuncta."

84. The latter, the personal presence of the Logos, by way of a mediated concomitance may arguably also entail, because of the circumincession of Father, Son, and Spirit, the personal presence of the Father and the Spirit. In regard to the theological status of such a proposal, I must admit that such a mediated concomitance has little if any textual support in Thomas and in later magisterial pronouncements. What stands against such a pronounced articulation of the mediated concomitance and hence of a real presence of the Trinity is the considerable danger of flattening out what is particular about the Eucharistic presence. During the period of Baroque Scholasticism, it seems that this position of mediated concomitance was held by Suárez, Vasquez, and Lugo, while it seems to have been rejected by the Salmanticenses, Billuart, and other Thomists. See Emmanuel Doronzo, *De Eucharistia*, 1:427–28. In more recent times, this mediated and extended concomitance was supported by Réginald Garrigou-Lagrange, OP, in his *De Eucharistia accedunt De Paenitentia quaestiones dogmaticae Commentarius in Summam theologicam S. Thomae* (Turin: Marietti, 1943), 148; and in principle we can find the position also in Matthias Joseph Scheeben, *The Mysteries of Christianity*, trans. Cyril Vollert, SJ (St. Louis, Mo.: Herder, 1951), 479–82. The spiritual implications of the mediated concomitance have been drawn out by M. V. Bernadot, OP, *From Holy Communion to the Blessed Trinity*, trans. Dom Francis Izard, OSB (Westminster, Md.: Newman Press, 1952).

85. *ST* III, q. 76, a. 3.

86. Ibid., obj. 2: "Corpus Christi, cum sit organicum, habet partes determinate distantes: est enim de ratione organici corporis determinata distantia singularum partium ad invicem, sicut oculi ab oculo, et oculi ab aure. Sed hoc non posset esse si sub qualibet parte specierum esset totus Christus: oporteret enim quod sub qualibet parte esset quaelibet pars; et ita, ubi esset una pars, esset et alia. Non ergo potest esse quod totus Christus sit sub qualibet parte hostiae vel vini contenti in calice."

87. *ST* III, q. 76, a. 3: "Because the substance of Christ's body is in this sacrament by the power of the sacrament, while dimensive quantity is there by reason of real concomitance, consequently Christ's body is in this sacrament substantively, that is, in the way in which substance is under dimensions, but not after the manner of dimensions, which means, not in the way in which the dimensive quantity of a body is under the dimensive quantity of place. Now it is evident that the whole nature of a substance is under every part of the dimensions under which it is contained; just as the entire nature of air is under every part of air, and the entire nature of bread under every part of bread; and this indifferently, whether the dimensions be actually divided (as when the air is divided or the bread cut), or whether they be actually undivided, but potentially divisible. And therefore it is manifest that the entire Christ is under every part of the species of the bread, even while the host remains entire, and not merely when it is broken, as some say, giving the example of an image which appears in a mirror, which appears as one in the unbroken mirror, whereas when the mirror is broken, there is an image in each part of the broken mirror: for the comparison is not perfect, because the multiplying of such images results in the broken mirror on account of the various reflections in the various parts of the mirror; but here there is only one consecration, whereby Christ's body is in this sacrament." (Corpus Christi est in hoc sacramento per modum substantiae, idest, per modum quo substantia est sub dimensionibus: non autem per modum dimensionum, idest, non per illum modum quo quantitatis dimensiva alicuius corporis est sub quantitate dimensiva loci. Manifestum est autem quod natura substantiae tota est sub qualibet parte dimensionum sub quibus continetur, sicut sub qualibet parte aeris est tota natura aeris, et sub qualibet parte panis est tota natura panis. Et hoc indifferenter sive dimensiones sint actu divisae, sicut cum aer dividitur vel panis secatur, vel etiam sint actu indivisae, divisibiles vero potentia. Et ideo manifestum est quod Christus totus est sub qualibet parte specierum panis, etiam hostia integra manente, et non solum cum frangitur, sicut quidam dicunt, ponentes exemplum de imagine quae apparet in speculo, quae una apparet in speculo integro, infracto autem speculo apparent

singulae in singulis partibus. Quod quidem non est omnino simile. Quia multiplicatio huiusmodi imaginum accidit in speculo fracto propter diversas reflexiones ad diversas partes speculi, hic autem non est nisi una consecratio propter quam corpus Christi est in sacramento.)

88. Journet, *The Mass*, 163.

89. *ST* III, q. 76, a. 3, ad 2: "Illa determinata distantia partium in corpore organico fundatur super quantitatem dimensivam ipsius; ipsa autem natura substantiae praecedit etiam quantitatem dimensivam. Et quia conversio substantiae panis directe terminatur ad substantiam corporis Christi, secundum cuius modum proprie et directe est in hoc sacramento corpus Christi, talis distantia partium est quidem in ipso corpore Christi vero, sed non secundum hanc distantiam comparatur ad hoc sacramentum, sed secundum modum suae substantiae."

90. *ST* III, q. 76, a. 4, s.c.: "Quantitas dimensiva corporis alicuius non separatur secundum esse a substantia eius. Sed in hoc sacramento est tota substantia corporis Christi.... Ergo tota quantitas dimensiva corporis Christi est in hoc sacramento."

91. *ST* III, q. 76, a. 4: "Quia tamen substantia corporis Christi realiter non denudatur a sua quantitate dimensiva et ab aliis accidentibus, inde est quod, ex vi realis concomitantiae, est in hoc sacramento tota quantitas dimensiva corporis Christi, et omnia alia accidentia eius."

92. *ST* III, q. 76, a. 4, ad 1: "Quia igitur ex vi sacramenti huius est in altari substantia corporis Christi, quantitas autem dimensiva eius est ibi concomitanter et quasi per accidens, ideo quantitas dimensiva corporis Christi est in hoc sacramento, non secundum proprium modum, ut scilicet sit totum in toto et singulae partes in singulis partibus; sed per modum substantiae, cuius natura est tota in toto et tota in qualibet parte." The backdrop of this argument is the very nature of the substantial form. The unity of substance dominates the multiplicity of parts. The substantial form is in every part of the material substance and constitutes thus the substantial unity. Thomas states in *ST* I, q. 76, a. 8: "Now the substantial form perfects not only the whole, but each part of the whole. For since a whole consists of parts, a form of the whole which does not give existence to each of the parts of the body, is a form consisting in composition and order, such as the form of a house; and such a form is accidental." (Substantialis autem forma non solum est perfectio totius, sed cuiuslibet partis. Cum enim totum consistat ex partibus, forma totius quae non dat esse singulis partibus corporis, est forma quae est compositio et ordo, sicut forma domus, et talis forma est accidentalis.) Cf. *In Meta.* VII, l. 2 (Marietti, no. 1277).

93. *ST* III, q. 76, a. 5: "Christ's body is in this sacrament not after the prop-

er manner of dimensive quantity, but rather after the manner of substance. But every body occupying a place is in the place according to the manner of dimensive quantity, namely, inasmuch as it is commensurate with the place according to its dimensive quantity. Hence it remains that Christ's body is not in this sacrament as in a place, but after the manner of substance, that is to say, in that way in which substance is contained by dimensions; because the substance of Christ's body succeeds the substance of bread in this sacrament: hence as the substance of bread was not locally under its dimensions, but after the manner of substance, so neither is the substance of Christ's body. Nevertheless the substance of Christ's body is not the subject of those dimensions, as was the substance of the bread: and therefore the substance of the bread was there locally by reason of its dimensions, because it was compared with that place through the medium of its own dimensions; but the substance of Christ's body is compared with that place through the medium of foreign dimensions, so that, on the contrary, the proper dimensions of Christ's body are compared with that place through the medium of substance; which is contrary to the notion of a located body." (Corpus Christi non est in hoc sacramento secundum proprium modum quantitatis dimensivae, sed magis secundum modum substantiae. Omne autem corpus locatum est in loco secundum modum quantitatis dimensivae, inquantum scilicet commensuratur loco secundum suam quantitatem dimensivam. Unde relinquitur quod corpus Christi non est in hoc sacramento sicut in loco, sed per modum substantiae, eo scilicet modo quo substantia continetur a dimensionibus. Succedit enim substantia corporis Christi in hoc sacramento substantiae panis. Unde, sicut substantia panis non erat sub suis dimensionibus localiter, sed per modum substantiae, ita nec substantia corporis Christi. Non tamen substantia corporis Christi est subiectum illarum dimensionum, sicut erat substantia panis. Et ideo panis ratione suarum dimensionum localiter erat ibi, quia comparabatur ad locum mediantibus propriis dimensionibus. Substantia autem corporis Christi comparatur ad locum illum mediantibus dimensionibus alienis, ita quod e converso dimensiones propriae corporis Christi comparantur ad locum illum mediante substantia. Quod est contra rationem corporis locati.)

94. *ST* III, q. 76, a. 5, ad 2: "Locus ille in quo est corpus Christi, non est vacuus. Neque tamen proprie est repletus substantia corporis Christi, quae non est ibi localiter, sicut dictum est. Sed est repletus speciebus sacramentorum, quae habent replere locum vel propter naturam dimensionum; vel saltem miraculose, sicut et miraculose subsistunt per modum substantiae."

95. Ibid., ad 3: "Accidentia corporis Christi sunt in hoc sacramento, sicut supra dictum est, secundum realem concomitantiam. Et ideo illa accidentia cor-

poris Christi sunt in hoc sacramento quae sunt ei intrinseca. Esse autem in loco est accidens per comparationem ad extrinsecum continens. Et ideo non oportet quod Christus sit in hoc sacramento sicut in loco."

96. For a detailed discussion of this particular aspect of Thomas's doctrine and of the sustainability of his teaching on the *accidentia sine subiecto remanentia*, see the instructive article by Petrus Sedlmayr, OSB, "Die Lehre des hl. Thomas von den accidentia *sine subiecto remanentia*—untersucht auf ihren Einklang mit der aristotelischen Philosophie," *Freiburger Zeitschrift für Philosophie und Theologie* 12 (1934): 315–26. Thomas is part of an intense philosophical discussion of this particularly complex question. For an excellent study that meticulously analyzes this discussion from early Scholasticism (Berengar and Lanfranc) up to Thomas Aquinas and the reaction to him by Godfrey of Fontaines, Aegidius Romanus, Dietrich of Freiberg, John of Paris, and John of Sterngassen, see Jörgen Vijgen, *The Status of Eucharistic Accidents "sine subiecto": An Historical Survey up to Thomas Aquinas and Selected Reactions* (Berlin: Akademieverlag, 2013); for a discussion of *ST* III, qq. 75 and 77, see 243–60. I am indebted to Vijgen's extraordinary study, the best on this crucial topic since the largely forgotten article by Petrus Sedlmayr.

97. The accounts of Olivi, Scotus, and Ockham can be usefully studied in David Burr's informative article "Quantity and Eucharistic Presence: The Debate from Olivi through Ockham," *Collectanea Franciscana* 44 (1974): 5–44. See more recently the instructive study by Marilyn McCord Adams, *Some Later Medieval Theories of the Eucharist: Thomas Aquinas, Giles of Rome, Duns Scotus, and William Ockham* (Oxford: Oxford University Press, 2010), a work whose strength rests in the lucid analysis of the differing philosophical accounts advanced and whose limitation consists in refraining to move from philosophical analysis to speculative contemplation, from the history of philosophy to sacred theology, to a contemplation that would integrate the biblical witness, the patrimony of the patristic period, and the doctrinal tradition of the church. Nevertheless, her study serves as a great aid in understanding what made possible conceptually the positions of Wycliffe, Luther, Zwingli, and Calvin, and what made necessary the doctrinal clarifications and specifications of the Council of Trent.

98. See Gordon Leff, *William of Ockham: The Metamorphosis of Scholastic Discourse* (Totowa, N.J.: Rowman and Littlefield, 1975), 207–13.

99. For an extensive analysis of the excruciatingly detailed discussion Ockham provides on this matter in his philosophical and theological works, see Erwin Iserloh, *Gnade und Eucharistie in der philosophischen Theologie des Wilhelm von Ockham: Ihre Bedeutung für die Ursachen der Reformation* (Steiner: Wies-

baden, 1956), 174–283, esp. 186–202 for a discussion of the problem in Ockham's commentary on Lombard's *Sentences* and 202–53 for a discussion of his position in his later *De sacramento altaris*. For a discussion of Ockham's doctrine more sympathetic than Iserloh's highly—and I think rightly—critical commentary, see Gabriel Buescher, OFM, *The Eucharistic Teaching of William Ockham* (St. Bonaventure, N.Y.: The Franciscan Institute, 1950), esp. 65–93.

100. René Descartes, *The Philosophical Writings of Descartes*, vol. 1: *Principles of Philosophy*, trans. John Cottingham, Robert Stoothoff, and Dugald Murdoch (Cambridge: Cambridge University Press, 1985), book 1, sections 48–53. Cf. esp. the following paradigmatic statements: "I recognize only two ultimate classes of things: first, intellectual or thinking things, i.e. those which pertain to mind or thinking substance; and secondly, material things, i.e., those which pertain to extended substance or body" (208, section 48). "A substance may indeed be known through any attribute at all; but each substance has one principal property which constitutes its nature and essence, and to which all its other properties are referred. Thus extension in length, breadth and depth constitutes the nature of corporeal substance; and thought constitutes the nature of thinking substance" (210, section 53).

101. Ibid., 226; part II, section 8.

102. "When they make a distinction between substance and extension or quantity, either they do not understand anything by the term 'substance,' or else they simply have a confused idea of the incorporeal substance, which they falsely attach to corporeal substance; and they relegate the true idea of corporeal substance to the category of extension, which, however, they term an accident. There is thus no correspondence between their verbal expression and what they grasp in their minds" (226; part II, section 9).

103. For details of this intricate and theologically not at all unproblematic position, see Jean-Robert Armogathe, *Theologia Cartesiana: L'explication physique de l'Eucharistie chez Descartes et dom Desgabets* (The Hague: Nijhoff, 1977), and his "Cartesian Physics and the Eucharist in the Documents of the Holy Office and the Roman Index (1671.6)," in *Receptions of Descartes: Cartesianism and Anti-Cartesianism in Early Modern Europe*, ed. Tad M. Schmaltz (New York: Routledge, 2005), 149–70; also Tad M. Schmaltz, *Radical Cartesianism: The French Reception of Descartes* (Cambridge: Cambridge University Press, 2002), esp. 34–74.

104. Joseph Gredt, *Logica: Philosophia Naturalis* (Freiburg: Herder, 1956), 145–46: "Definitio quantitatis ... stricte autem sumpta pro quantitate *praedicamentali* definitur: ordo partium in toto. In qua definitione 'ordo' posititionem significat partium extra partes, ita ut quantitas etiam definiri possit: accidens

tribuens subiecto habere partes extra partes quoad se. Ordo, in quo consistit quantitatis essentia, non est relatio ordinis, sed fundamentum huius relationis; est ordo fundamentalis, i.e., fundamentum relationis secundum prius et posterius. Quantitas igitur duo continet: *multitudinem* partium, et huius multitudinis *ordinem* secundum positionem, quatenus partes ponuntur extra partes secundum prius et posterius.... Quare quantitas praedicamentalis multitudini superaddit ordinem positionis secundum prius et posterius." Ibid., 252: "THESIS X: Effectus formalis primarius quantitatis seu eius ratio formalis est ordo partium in toto, effectus formalis secundarius est ubi et situs seu ordo partium in loco. Hic effectus secundarius distinctus est realiter et separabilis a primario." Ibid., 252 (§315): "*Effectus formalis primarius* seu ratio formalis est constitutivum metaphysicum quantitatis. Quantitas enim utpote accidens definitur per ordinem ad subiectum, ad substantiam. Quare indicando, quid *primo* faciat in substantia formaliter (per modum causae formalis), indicatur eius essentia metaphysica." Ibid., 254 (§318): "ordo partium in toto potest considerari indeterminate, et tunc est *effectus formalis primarius* quantitatis."

105. *ST* I, q. 90, a. 2: "Now that properly exists which itself has existence; as it were, subsisting in its own existence. Wherefore only substances are properly and truly called beings; whereas an accident has not existence, but something is (modified) by it, and so far is it called a being; for instance, whiteness is called a being, because by it something is white. Hence it is said in *Metaph.* vii that an accident should be described as 'of something rather than as something.' The same is to be said of all non-subsistent forms." (Illud autem proprie dicitur esse, quod ipsum habet esse, quasi in suo esse subsistens: unde solae substantiae proprie et vere dicuntur entia. Accidens vero non habet esse, sed eo aliquid est, et hac ratione ens dicitur; sicut albedo dicitur ens, quia ea aliquid est album. Et propter hoc dicitur in VII *Metaphys.*, quod accidens dicitur "magis entis quam ens." Et eadem ratio est de omnibus aliis formis non subsistentibus.)

106. Hence, it is crucial to remember that, when Thomas distinguishes between substance and quantity in *ST* III, q. 76, a. 1, ad 3, he is concerned with the specific entailments of the *ordo partium* in space, that is, the secondary formal effect of quantity, the order of the parts in the place (*ordo partium in loco*) and with it the position or situation of the parts under consideration relative to other parts in space (*ubi et situs*). Consider his argument in *ST* III, q. 76, a. 1, ad 3: "As has been already stated [q. 75, a. 5], after the consecration of the bread into the body of Christ, or of the wine into His blood, the accidents of both remain. From which it is evident that the dimensions of the bread or wine are not changed into the dimensions of the body of Christ, but substance into substance. And so the substance of Christ's body or blood is under this sacra-

ment by the power of the sacrament, but not the dimensions of Christ's body or blood. Hence it is clear that the body of Christ is in this sacrament 'by way of substance,' and not by way of quantity. But the proper totality of substance is contained indifferently in a small or large quantity; as the whole nature of air in a great or small amount of air, and the whole nature of a [human being] in a big or small individual. Wherefore, after the consecration, the whole substance of Christ's body and blood is contained in this sacrament, just as the whole substance of the bread and wine was contained there before the consecration." (Sicut dictum est, facta conversione panis in corpus Christi vel vini in sanguinem, accidentia utriusque remanent. Ex quo patet quod dimensiones panis vel vini non convertuntur in dimensiones corporis Christi, sed substantia in substantiam. Et sic substantia corporis Christi vel sanguinis est in hoc sacramento ex vi sacramenti, non autem dimensiones corporis vel sanguinis Christi. Unde patet quod corpus Christi est in hoc sacramento per modum substantiae, et non per modum quantitatis. Propria autem totalitas substantiae continetur indifferenter in parva vel magna quantitate, sicut tota natura aeris in magno vel parvo aere, et tota natura hominis in magno vel parvo homine. Unde et tota substantia corporis Christi et sanguinis continetur in hoc sacramento post consecrationem, sicut ante consecrationem continebatur ibi substantia panis et vini.)

107. *ST* III, q. 75, a. 5, ad 1: "As is said in the book *De Causis*, an effect depends more on the first cause than on the second. And therefore by God's power, which is the first cause of all things, it is possible for that which follows to remain, while that which is first is taken away." (Sicut dicitur in libro *De causis*, effectus plus dependet a causa prima quam a causa secunda. Et ideo virtute Dei, qui est causa prima omnium, fieri potest ut remaneant posteriora, sublatis prioribus.) See also John of St. Thomas, *Cursus philosophicus Thomisticus* I, Log., part II, q. XVI, a. 1 (463): "Caeterum oppositum hujus manifestavit nobis sacrosanctum Eucharistiae mysterium, in quo manet quantitas, quae antea erat panis, ut oculis videmus, et non manet substantia panis, ut fides docet: distinguitur ergo et separatur quantitas a re quanta. Respondent Nominales quantitatem substantiae non manere, cum ipsa enim evanuit; sed manere quantitatem qualitatum caeterorumque accidentium extensorum. Sed contra est, quia ibi sunt plura accidentia. Vel ergo unumquodque habet suam quantitatem distinctam, vel datur aliqua communis omnibus. Si datur aliqua communis omnibus, illa distinguitur ab unoquoque accidente, cum sit communis pluribus; et distinguitur etiam a substantia, quae ibi non est; ergo distinguitur quantitas a re quanta."

108. Cf. Thomas's nuanced discussion of this complex matter in *ST* III, q. 77, a. 2: "It is necessary to say that the other accidents which remain in this sacrament are subjected in the dimensive quantity of the bread and wine that

remains: first of all, because something having quantity and color and affected by other accidents is perceived by the senses; nor is sense deceived in such.
Secondly, because the first disposition of matter is dimensive quantity, hence
Plato also assigned 'great' and 'small' as the first differences of matter (Aristotle,
Metaph. iv). And because the first subject is matter, the consequence is that all
other accidents are related to their subject through the medium of dimensive
quantity; just as the first subject of color is said to be the surface, on which account some have maintained that dimensions are the substances of bodies, as is
said in *Metaph.* iii. And since, when the subject is withdrawn, the accidents remain according to the being which they had before, it follows that all accidents
remain founded upon dimensive quantity. Thirdly, because, since the subject is
the principle of individuation of the accidents, it is necessary for what is admit-
ted as the subject of some accidents to be somehow the principle of individuation: for it is of the very notion of an individual that it cannot be in several; and
this happens in two ways. First, because it is not natural to it to be in any one;
and in this way immaterial separated forms, subsisting of themselves, are also
individuals of themselves. Secondly, because a form, be it substantial or accidental, is naturally in someone indeed, not in several, as this whiteness, which is
in this body. As to the first, matter is the principle of individuation of all inherent forms, because, since these forms, considered in themselves, are naturally
in something as in a subject, from the very fact that one of them is received in
matter, which is not in another, it follows that neither can the form itself thus
existing be in another. As to the second, *it must be maintained that the principle
of individuation is dimensive quantity. For that something is naturally in another one
solely, is due to the fact that that other is undivided in itself, and distinct from all others. But it is on account of quantity that substance can be divided, as is said in Phys.
i. And therefore dimensive quantity itself is a particular principle of individuation in
forms of this kind, namely, inasmuch as forms numerically distinct are in different
parts of the matter. Hence also dimensive quantity has of itself a kind of individuation, so that we can imagine several lines of the same species, differing in position, which is included in the notion of this quantity; for it belongs to dimension for it to be 'quantity having position'* (Aristotle, *Categor.* iv), and therefore
dimensive quantity can be the subject of the other accidents, rather than the
other way about" (emphasis added).

　　109. Translation from Saint Thomas Aquinas, *Summa Contra Gentiles, Book
Four: Salvation*, trans. Charles J. O'Neil (Notre Dame, Ind.: University of Notre
Dame Press, 1975), 262. *Summa Contra Gentiles* [hereafter *SCG*] IV.64.5: "Corpus enim Christi per suas proprias dimensiones in uno tantum loco existit: sed
mediantibus dimensionibus panis in ipsum transeuntis in tot locis in quot hui-

usmodi conversio fuerit celebrata: non quidem divisum per partes, sed integrum in unoquoque; nam quilibet panis consecratus in integrum corpus Christi convertitur."

110. Author's translation from *Sancti Thomae Aquinatis Doctoris Angelici
Opera Omnia iussu edita Leonis XIII P.M.* (Rome: Commissio Leonina, 1926),
15:208: "Duplex est quantitatis effectus. Unus est omnino intrinsecus subiecto
quanto; scilicet esse quantum, et divisibilitas in partes, atque ordo partium in
toto. Alius est aliquo modo extrinsecus, inquantum scilicet convenit subiecto
in ordine ad extrinsecum; scilicet condividi alteri quantitati, et partes eius partibus loci correspondere. Primum convenit quantitati necessario et per se: secundum vero sibi non convenit nisi quando habet primo et per se ordinem ad
locum et ad extrinsecas dimensiones. In sacramento ergo Altaris quantitas corporis Christi, sub dimensionibus panis existens, habet primum effectum, quia
ipsum corpus Christi est in seipso divisibile, et habet ordinem partium in toto:
non autem secundum effectum habet, quia partes corporis Christi non corres-
pondent partibus dimensionis panis neque partibus loci, sed totum est sub qualibet parte. Ex quo sequitur quod potest dici corpus Christi esse sub dimensionibus panis et divisibiliter et indivisibiliter; divisibiliter quidem, quia in seipso
divisibilitatem partium habet; indivisibiliter autem, quia partes eius non corres-
pondent partibus illarum dimensionum, sed totum cuilibet parti, sicut anima
est tota in qualibet parte."

111. *Decree on the Most Holy Eucharist*, c. 1.

112. Ibid.

113. Cf. Pope Leo XIII, *Mirae Caritatis*, Encyclical Letter, in *Acta Leonis XIII*
22 (1902–3): 123.

114. Cf. Council of Trent, *Decree on the Most Holy Eucharist*, c. 4 and canon 2.

115. At this point I cannot delve into all the arresting details of Thomas's
demanding metaphysical interpretation of the mystery of Eucharistic conversion. Stephen Brock, in his essay, "St. Thomas and the Eucharistic Conversion,"
The Thomist 65, no. 4 (2001): 529–65, has provided such an extraordinarily su-
perb account of Thomas's argument that I happily refer interested readers to his
work. Those students and connoisseurs of Thomas's philosophy of being who
might have missed in my discussion so far any treatment of the act of being
(*actus essendi*) will find in Brock's article what they might look for in vain here.
For it is the metaphysical contemplation of substantial conversion that indeed
makes a consideration of the act of being indispensable. As, however, I focus in
this discussion exclusively on the terminus of the conversion, Christ's real, corporeal presence—the metaphysical concepts of "substance" and "accident" (or

"species") suffice. In short, not having mentioned the act of being extensively does not mean that I do not regard it as absolutely indispensable for a full metaphysical consideration of substantial conversion. To the contrary; being (*esse*) is act, the fulness of actuality (*actus*), which is the perfection of all perfections. As form gives being (*forma dat esse*), the substantial form of a being (*ens*) is its act of being (*actus essendi*). By way of the act of being, each created finite being (*ens per participationem*) participates the gift of being (*ipsum esse creatum*), that is, the first creature, so to speak, and the closest created similitude of the uncreated divine essence (*ens or esse per essentiam*). As the plenitude of actuality (*actus*), *ipsum esse creatum* is *simplex et completum*. It does not subsist independently, but as the participated gift received by the participating act of being as limited by the principle of essence, that is, as substance. A substance is *ens per se*, because it has being in virtue of the act of being. It realizes itself by way of the act of being according to its nature. The substantial conversion occurs on the ontological level of the act of being.

116. John of St. Thomas, *Cursus philosophicus Thomisticus* I, Log., part II, q. XVI, a. 1 (466): "In sententia S. Thomae propria et formalis ratio quantitatis est extensio partium in ordine ad totum, quod est reddere partes formaliter integrantes. Unde remota quantitate, substantia non habet partes integrales formaliter in ratione partis ordinatas et distinctas."

117. For an extensive discussion of this crucial aspect of Thomas's Christology, see Theophil Tschipke, OP, *Die Menschheit Christi als Heilsorgan der Gottheit unter besonderer Berücksichtigung der Lehre des heiligen Thomas von Aquin* (Freiburg: Herder, 1940), or the French translation by Philibert Secrétan: *L'humanité du Christ comme instrument de salut de la divinité* (Fribourg: Academic Press, 2003).

118. Lest I be misunderstood to claim that this developed Thomist position is necessarily intended by or even entailed in the church's teaching on Eucharistic conversion, allow me to cite the words of one from whom such sobering warning and restraint in judgment might these days be least expected. The following comment is made in response to the question "Is the distinction between two functions of quantity at all necessary?" (Haec distinctio duarum functionum quantitatis estne omnino necessaria?): "For the science of theology the terminology used by St. Thomas in our article actually suffices; that is, the dimensive quantity of Christ's body is in this sacrament not according to its proper manner ... but after the manner of substance.... This terminology suffices and in these surpassingly difficult matters one must 'be wise unto sobriety' [*sapere ad sobrietatem*; Rom 12:3, Vulgate and Douay-Rheims], for the will to excessive explication leads to a false subtlety, to a 'minute accuracy' [*acribo-*

logia], as Aristotle calls it, which distracts from the contemplation of the mysteries.... St. Thomas, who generally corrected his manuscripts by contracting them and not by developing them further, brilliantly observed this sobriety, more so than most of his commentators, who sometimes want to explicate his teaching too much by way of lower things without sufficiently pursuing the contemplation of loftier things." Réginald Garrigou-Lagrange, OP, *De Eucharistia*, 146–47 (author's translation). Faced with an intellectual context shaped by Olivi, Scotus, Ockham, and eventually Descartes, Thomist commentators were led to go beyond what Garrigou-Lagrange, under different intellectual circumstances, rightly regards as the wisely restrained and indeed sufficient terminology of Thomas Aquinas.

119. A complicated issue that goes beyond the scope of this study is thematized by the question of whether the Eucharist is one substance or two substances. A decree of the Council of Trent states: "the conversion of the whole substance of the bread into the substance of the body of Christ our Lord, and of the whole substance of the wine into the substance of his blood." Council of Trent, thirteenth session (October 11, 1551), chap. 4, "De transsubstantiatione," in *Decrees* (ed. Tanner), 2:695. From this phrasing, it might seem that the Eucharist is two substances. However, in Thomas's teaching there is a marked tendency to simply state that the result of the transubstantiation is "the whole Christ." One might consider here especially Thomas's statement (noting the numbers) in *ST* III, q. 76, a. 1, ad 3: "After the consecration of the bread into the body of Christ, or of the wine into His blood, the accidents of both remain. From which it is evident that the dimensions of the bread or wine are not changed into the dimensions of the body of Christ, but *substance into substance. And so the substance of Christ's body or blood is under this sacrament by the power of the sacrament, but not the dimensions of Christ's body or blood.* Hence it is clear that the body of Christ is in this sacrament 'by way of substance,' and not by way of quantity. But the proper totality of substance is contained indifferently in a small or large quantity; as the whole nature of air in a great or small amount of air, and the whole nature of a man in a big or small individual. Wherefore, after the consecration, *the whole substance of Christ's body and blood* is contained in this sacrament, just as the whole substance of the bread and wine was contained there before the consecration" (emphasis added). (Facta conversione panis in corpus Christi vel vini in sanguinem, accidentia utriusque remanent. Ex quo patet quod dimensiones panis vel vini non convertuntur in dimensiones corporis Christi, sed substantia in substantiam. Et sic substantia corporis Christi vel sanguinis est in hoc sacramento ex vi sacramenti, non autem dimensiones corporis vel sanguinis Christi. Unde patet quod corpus Christi est in hoc sacra-

mento per modum substantiae, et non per modum quantitatis. Propria autem
totalitas substantiae continetur indifferenter in parva vel magna quantitate, sicut tota natura aeris in magno vel parvo aere, et tota natura hominis in magno
vel parvo homine. Unde et tota substantia corporis Christi et sanguinis continetur in hoc sacramento post consecrationem, sicut ante consecrationem continebatur ibi substantia panis et vini.) Based on Thomas's teaching and despite
the Tridentine language, there are more recent Thomist theologians who seem
to suggest that the Eucharist is one substance, not two substances. See Emmanuel Doronzo, OMI, *De Eucharistia*, 1:425; Louis Billot, SJ, *De Ecclesiae Sacramentis*, 1:482, esp. 484; and implicitly in some of the material in Garrigou-Lagrange, *De Eucharistia*, 132. I am indebted to Fr. Dominic Langevin, OP, for
bringing this complicated issue to my attention.

CHAPTER 4

120. *ST* III, q. 62, a. 6: "Sicut enim ex praedictis patet, virtus passionis
Christi copulatur nobis per fidem et sacramenta, differenter tamen: nam continuatio quae est per fidem, fit per actum animae; continuatio autem quae est
per sacramenta, fit per usum exteriorum rerum."

121. *ST* III, q. 62, a. 5: "Manifestum est autem ex his quae supra dicta sunt,
quod Christus liberavit nos a peccatis nostris praecipue per suam passionem,
non solum efficienter et meritorie, sed etiam satisfactorie. Similiter etiam per
suam passionem initiavit ritum Christianae religionis, 'offerens seipsum obla-
tionem et hostiam Deo,' ut dicitur *Ephes.* 5, [2]. Unde manifestum est quod sacramenta Ecclesiae specialiter habent virtutem ex passione Christi, cuius virtus
quodammmodo nobis copulatur per susceptionem sacramentorum. In cuius
signum, de latere Chrisi pendentis in cruce fluxerunt aqua et sanguis, quorum
unum pertinet ad baptismum, aliud ad Eucharistiam, quae sunt potissima sacramenta."

122. *ST* III, q. 62, a. 1, ad 1 (emphasis added): "The principal cause cannot
properly be called a sign of its effect, even though the latter be hidden and the
cause itself sensible and manifest. *But an instrumental cause, if manifest, can be
called a sign of a hidden effect, for this reason, that it is not merely a cause but also in
a measure an effect in so far as it is moved by the principal agent. And in this sense
the sacraments of the New Law are both cause and signs.* Hence, too, is it that, to
use the common expression, '*they effect what they signify.*' From this it is clear
that they perfectly fulfil the conditions of a sacrament; being ordained to something sacred, not only as a sign, but also as a cause." For two illuminating studies of the Thomist understanding of the sacraments as signs that are inherently
instrumental causes, see Humbert Bouëssé, OP, "La causalité efficiente instru-

mentale de l'humanité du Christ et des sacraments chrétiens," *Revue Thomiste* 39 (1934): 33–57, and Reginald Lynch, OP, *The Cleansing of the Heart: The Sacraments as Instrumental Causes in the Thomistic Tradition* (Washington, D.C.: The Catholic University of America Press, 2017).

123. For an excellent treatment, to which I am greatly indebted in this section, see Benoît-Dominique de La Soujeole, OP, "The Importance of the Definition of Sacraments as Signs," in *Ressourcement Thomism: Sacred Doctrine, the Sacraments, and the Moral Life*, ed. Reinhard Hütter and Matthew Levering (Washington, D.C.: The Catholic University of America Press, 2010), 127–35.

124. Anscar Vonier, OSB, *A Key to the Doctrine of the Eucharist* (Bethesda, Md.: Zaccheus, 2003), 21.

125. Denzinger, no. 690: "scilicet panem et vinum, quae in altari ponuntur, post consecrationem non solum sacramentum, sed etiam verum corpus et sanguinem Domini nostri Iesu Christi esse, et sensualiter, non solum sacramento, sed in veritate, manibus sacerdotum tractari et frangi et fidelium dentibus atteri." The English translation of this section provided by Robert Fastiggi and Anne Englund Nash in the bilingual Denziger-Hünermann edition renders the passage thus: "namely, that the bread and wine that are placed on the altar, after the consecration, are not only a sacrament, but also the true Body and Blood of our Lord Jesus Christ and that they are sensibly, not only in sacrament but in truth, touched and broken by the hands of priests and ground by the teeth of the faithful" (Denzinger, no. 690). Cardinal Humbert's pronounced physicalism—an extreme interpretation of the position of Carolingian theologian and Benedictine abbot Paschasius Radbertus (785–865)—stands in marked tension to the Augustinian tradition. On the Augustinian nature of Berengar's doctrine, see Irène Rosier-Catach, *La parole efficace: Signe, rituel, sacré* (Paris: Editions du Seuil, 2004), 36–40. On the leaders of the opposition to and tracts directed against Berengar, see Geiselmann, *Die Eucharistielehre der Vorscholastiker*, and Henry Chadwick, "Ego Berengarius," *Journal of Theological Studies* 40, no. 2 (1989): 414–45.

126. Those who would like to understand Thomas's proper prioritization of sacramental signification as a subtle acknowledgment of aspects of truth in Berengar's doctrine may want to recall Thomas's explicit and unambiguous reference to Berengar at the very end of the corpus of *ST* III, q. 75, a. 1: "Some men accordingly, not paying heed to these things, have contended that Christ's body and blood are not in this sacrament except as in a sign, a thing to be rejected as heretical, since it is contrary to Christ's words. Hence Berengarius, who had been the first deviser of this heresy, was afterwards forced to withdraw his error, and to acknowledge the truth of the faith." The one who explicitly adopted Berengar's doctrine was none other than John Wycliffe. For Wycliffe's precise un-

derstanding of the doctrine of transubstantiation, of which he gives an accurate definition, see Engelbert Gutwenger, SJ, "Substanz und Akzidenz in der Eucharistielehre," *Zeitschrift für Katholische Theologie* 83 (1961): 257–306, at 269n36.

127. Arguably, for Thomas *res tantum* can be achieved by the simple celebration of Mass (even without Eucharistic communion), which for him is essentially the consecration.

128. Fr. Dominic Langevin, OP, made the case (personal communication, January 17, 2018) that the signification and efficacy of the *sacramentum tantum* extends not just to the *res et sacramentum* but also to the *res tantum*. He argued that with respect to Thomas's Eucharistic theology, one can see this dynamic when the angelic doctor discusses the *sacramentum tantum* in *ST* III, q. 73: a number of the thoughts concerning the signification actually do relate to the *res tantum* and not just to the *res et sacramentum* (e.g., the many grains of wheat making up the one bread are a sign of the united mystical Body of Christ).

129. Vonier, *Key to the Doctrine of the Eucharist*, 49.

130. *ST* III, q. 76, a. 2, ad 1: "Quamvis totus Christus sit sub utraque specie, non tamen frustra. Nam primo quidem, hoc valet ad repraesentandam passionem Christi, in qua seorsum sanguis fuit a corpore. Unde et in forma consecrationis sanguinis fit mentio de eius effusione. Secundo, hoc est conveniens usui huius sacramenti, ut seorsum exhibeatur fidelibus corpus Christi in cibum, et sanguis in potum. Tertio, quantum ad effectum, secundum quod supra dictum est quod 'corpus exhibetur pro salute corporis, sanguis pro salute animae.'"

131. On this crucial matter see Thierry-Dominique Humbrecht, OP, "L'eucharistie, 'représentation' du sacrifice du Christ selon Saint Thomas," *Revue Thomiste* 98, no. 3 (1998): 355–86.

132. Thomas Aquinas, *In De generatione* 1.8 (62 [5]): "No substantial form is *per se* perceptible to sense; but to the intellect alone, whose object is the 'what something is,' as is said in *On the Soul* III. The forms that are *per se* perceptible to sense are qualities of the third type, called for this reason, 'passible,' since they cause passions in the senses, as is said in the *Predicaments*." In *Exposition of Aristotle's Treatise on Generation and Corruption, Book I, cc. 1–5*, trans. Pierre Conway, OP, and R. F. Larcher, OP (Columbus, Ohio: College of St. Mary of the Springs, 1964).

133. *ST* II-II, q. 8, a. 1 (trans. Lawrence Dewan, "The Importance of Substance," in *Form and Being*, 118): "Nomen intellectus quandam intimam cognitionem importat, dicitur enim intelligere quasi 'intus legere.' Et hoc manifeste patet considerantibus differentiam intellectus et sensus, nam cognitio sensitiva occupatur circa qualitates sensibiles exteriores; cognitio autem intellectiva penetrat usque ad essentiam rei, obiectum enim intellectus est 'quod quid est,'

ut dicitur in III *De anima*. Sunt autem multa genera eorum quae interius latent, ad quae oportet cognitionem hominis quasi intrinsecus penetrare. Nam sub accidentibus latet natura rerum substantialis, sub verbis latent significata verborum, sub similitudinibus et figuris latet veritas figurata: res etiam intelligibiles sunt quodammodo interiores respectu rerum sensibilium quae exterius sentiuntur, et in causis latent effectus et e converso. Unde respectu horum omnium potest dici intellectus."

134. *ST* III, q. 76, a. 7: "Substantia autem, inquantum huiusmodi, non est visibilis oculo corporali, neque subiacet alicui sensui, neque imaginationi, sed soli intellectui, cuius obiectum est 'quod quid est,' ut dicitur in III *De anima*. Et ideo, proprie loquendo, corpus Christi, secundum modum essendi quem habet in hoc sacramento: neque sensu neque imaginatione perceptibile est, sed solo intellectu, qui dicitur oculus spiritualis." He continues: "Consequently the devils cannot by their intellect perceive Christ in this sacrament, except through faith, to which they do not pay willing assent; yet they are convinced from the evidence of signs, according to James 2:19: 'The devils believe, and tremble.'" (Unde daemones non possunt videre per intellectum Christum in hoc sacramento, nisi per fidem: cui non voluntate assentiunt, sed ad eam signorum evidentia convincuntur, prout dicitur, *Iac*. 2, [19], quod "daemones credunt et contremiscunt.") See also *In de An.* II, l. 14 (Marietti, no. 420).

135. *ST* III, q. 76, a. 7.

136. *ST* III, q. 75, a. 5, ad 2 and 3: "In hoc sacramento nulla est deceptio: sunt enim secundum rei veritatem accidentia, quae sensibus diiudicantur. Intellectus autem, cuius est proprium obiectum substantia, ut dicitur in *III De anima*, per fidem a deceptione praeservatur."

137. *ST* II-II, q. 2, a. 9: "Ipsum autem credere est actus intellectus assentientis veritati divinae ex imperio voluntatis a Deo motae per gratiam."

138. *ST* II-II, q. 1, a. 2, ad 2: "Actus autem credentis non terminatur ad enuntiabile, sed ad rem: non enim formamus enuntiabilia, nisi ut per ea de rebus cognitionem habeamus, sicut in scientia, ita et in fide." In an unjustly forgotten but still highly important document, the International Theological Commission reminds us that this is not Thomas's personal opinion but indeed the church's teaching: "All revelation ultimately is the self-revelation and self-communication by God the Father through the Son in the Holy Spirit, so that we may have communion with God (*Dei Verbum*, no. 2). God is therefore the one and all-encompassing object of faith and theology (Thomas Aquinas). Therefore the following is true: 'The act of the believer comes to its term not in a formula but in a reality' (ST II-II, q. 1, a. 2, ad 2)." International Theological Commission, "On the Interpretation of Dogmas," 9.

139. *ST* I, q. 13, a. 1: "It follows therefore that we can give a name to anything in as far as we can understand it." (Secundum igitur quod aliquid a nobis intellectu cognosci potest, sic a nobis potest nominari.) In our particular
case of faith's assent, though, the naming is received first, *solo auditu*, and sub-
sequently, a knowing occurs, but an "obscure knowing," precisely because it is
received *solo auditu*.

140. Brock, "St. Thomas and the Eucharistic Conversion," 556.

141. *De malo*, q. 1, a. 3, ad 11: "Fides non est meritoria ex hoc quod est cognitio enigmatica, set ex hoc quod tali cognitione uoluntas bene utitur, assentien-
do scilicet his que non uidet propter Deum." Text and translation from *The De
Malo of Thomas Aquinas*, ed. Brian Davies, trans. Richard Regan (Oxford: Oxford University Press, 2001), 90–91. In this particular response to an objection,
Thomas accounts for the fact that a deficient vision (i.e., a "malum") can be the
cause of merit. The key is that faith is meritorious insofar as the will uses the
obscure knowledge by assenting to unseen things for God's sake.

142. *The Aquinas Prayer Book*, 68–69. Regarding the authenticity of this
hymn, see Torrell, *Saint Thomas Aquinas*, 1:132–35, and also Tück, *A Gift of Presence*, 229–31. For Tück's illuminating and edifying theological interpretation of
the hymn, see *A Gift of Presence*, 232–43. He shows convincingly how the hymn
is a surpassingly beautiful and perfectly fitting poetic expression of Thomas's
Eucharistic theology.

143. While I remain uncertain whether the alternatives indeed are the right
ones, if one accepts the parameters set in the famous extended debate of the
1950s between Filippo Selvaggi and Carlo Colombo, I indeed tend toward the
position of the latter. See Gutwenger, "Substanz und Akzidenz," 283–304, for an
instructive exposition and summary of this debate. More accessible to an En-
glish-speaking readership are the articles by Joseph T. Clark, SJ, "Physics, Philosophy, Transubstantiation, Theology," *Theological Studies* 12, no. 1 (1951): 24–
51 (describing the first stage of the debate between Selvaggi and Colombo), and
Cyril Vollert, SJ, "The Eucharist: Controversy on Transubstantiation," *Theological Studies* 22, no. 3 (1961): 391–425 (describing the second stage of the debate). See also the quite brilliant and thought-provoking articles by Richard G.
Cipolla (PhD in chemistry from the University of Rhode Island and D.Phil in
theology from Oxford University), "Selvaggi Revisited: Transubstantiation and
Contemporary Science," *Theological Studies* 35, no. 4 (1974): 667–91. According
to Cipolla's lucid description, Selvaggi (whose first article appeared in the Gre-
gorianum in 1949) holds the view that "modern physics does indeed force the
theologian to take a look at transubstantiation and to be at least willing to talk
about this doctrine in the categories and thought-forms of modern physics.
Having laid down this basic principle—a principle which should not be tak-

en for granted and has far-reaching implications—Selvaggi proceeds to carry out a remythologizing of the doctrine of transubstantiation in terms of modern physical conceptions of reality. If contemporary physicists see things as made up of molecules, atoms, electrons, mesons, etc., the theologian must explain what he means by transubstantiation in terms of the same molecules, atoms, etc. Selvaggi proceeds to do just that" (668). In 1955, Colombo, according to Cipolla's summary, "takes Selvaggi to task for attempting to do the impossible: to 'explain' transubstantiation in terms of contemporary science. He demonstrates how others since Descartes have made this attempt and have failed, for the physics upon which their explanation of transubstantiation was based had changed with new advances in science. Why Selvaggi's view is both impossible and improper is because, according to Colombo, in transubstantiation we are dealing with a purely metaphysical change as opposed to a physical change. The reality of the substance of the bread, as well as of the body of Christ, is a metaphysical reality and as such is completely beyond the scope of the physical scientist, who is concerned with the accidental character, or species, of things. The scientist concerns himself with measurements, with tracking electrons, with infrared spectroscopy. He is not concerned with ontological reality but merely phenomenal, i.e., accidental reality. Thus the conversion of the bread and wine to the body and blood of Christ has nothing to do with the 'reality' talked about by the physicist, for metaphysical reality and physical reality are quite distinct and irreducible to each other" (669).

144. *ST* III, q. 76, a. 7, co.

145. *ST* III, q. 75, a. 1: "Hoc competit perfectioni fidei, quae, sicut est de divinitate Christi, ita est de eius humanitate: secundum illud *Ioan.* 14, [1]: 'Creditis in Deum, et in me credite.' Et quia fides est invisibilium, sicut divinitatem suam nobis exhibet Christus invisibiliter, ita et in hoc sacramento carnem suam nobis exhibit invisibili modo."

CHAPTER 5

146. *ST* III, q. 75, a. 1. Thomas cites here from Aristotle's *Nicomachean Ethics* IX.12, 1171b32: "This belongs to Christ's love, out of which for our salvation He assumed a true body of our nature. And because it is the special feature of friendship to live together with friends, as the Philosopher says (*Ethic.* ix), He promises us His bodily presence as a reward, saying (Mt 24:28): 'Where the body is, there shall the eagles be gathered together.' Yet meanwhile in our pilgrimage He does not deprive us of His bodily presence; but unites us with Himself in this sacrament through the truth of His body and blood. Hence (Jn 6:57) he says: 'He that eateth My flesh, and drinketh My blood, abideth in Me,

and I in him.' Hence this sacrament is the sign of supreme charity, and the up-lifter of our hope, from such familiar union of Christ with us."

147. *ST* III, q. 75, a. 1.

148. Ibid.: "Interim tamen nec sua praesentia corporali in hac peregrinati-one destituit, sed per veritatem corporis et sanguinis sui nos sibi coniungit in hoc sacramento."

149. *ST* III, q. 73, a. 3: "Res sacramenti est unitas corporis mystici."

150. On rightly distinguishing between Christ's mystical body and the visi-ble church without separating the one from the other, see *ST* III, q. 8, a. 3.

151. *ST* III, q. 80, a. 4: "Quicumque ergo hoc sacramentum sumit, ex hoc ipso significat se esse Christo unitum et membris eius incorporatum. Quod quidem fit per fidem formatam, quam nullus habet cum peccato mortali. Et ideo manifestum est quod quicumque cum peccato mortali hoc sacramentum sumit, falsitatem in hoc sacramento committit. Et ideo incurrit sacrilegium, tan-quam sacramenti violator. Et propter hoc mortaliter peccat."

152. For inroads into Thomas's rich ecclesiology, hidden and diffused throughout his corpus and accessible to a large degree only by way of his Chris-tology, pneumatology, and sacramentology, see Yves Congar, OP, "The Idea of the Church in St. Thomas Aquinas," *The Thomist* 1, no. 3 (1939): 331–59; reprint-ed with revisions in his *The Mystery of the Church* (Baltimore, Md.: Helicon Press, 1960), 53–74. For a more recent insightful overview, see George Sabra, *Thomas Aquinas' Vision of the Church: Fundamentals of an Ecumenical Ecclesi-ology* (Mainz: Grünewald, 1987), and the informative chapter by Thomas F. O'Meara, OP, "Theology of the Church," in *The Theology of Thomas Aquinas*, ed. Rik van Nieuwenhove and Joseph Wawrykow (Notre Dame, Ind.: Univer-sity of Notre Dame Press, 2005), 303–25.

153. Henri de Lubac, *Corpus Mysticum: The Eucharist and the Church in the Middle Ages*, ed. Laurence Paul Hemming and Susan Frank Parsons, trans. Gemma Simmonds, CJ, Richard Price, and Christopher Stephens (Notre Dame, Ind.: University of Notre Dame Press, 2006), 261.

154. See Thomas's discussion in *ST* III, q. 80, and the Council of Trent's ex-plicit statement in canon 4 of the "Decree on the Sacrament of the Eucharist" in Denzinger, no. 1654.

155. Henri de Lubac, *Catholicism: Christ and the Common Destiny of Man*, trans. Lancelot C. Sheppard and Sr. Elizabeth Englund, OCD (San Francisco: Ignatius Press, 1988), 319.

156. This famous phrase was coined by Henri de Lubac, SJ, in his 1944 study *Corpus Mysticum*. It appears in the context of de Lubac's description of how early medieval theologians understood the body of Christ to be enlivened by the Spir-it, how the ecclesial body becomes in reality the body of Christ: "Now, the Eu-

charist is the mystical principle, permanently at work at the heart of the Christian society, which gives concrete form to this miracle. It is the universal bond, it is the ever-springing source of life. Nourished by the body and blood of the Saviour, his faithful people thus all 'drink of the one Spirit,' who truly makes them into one single body. *Literally speaking, therefore, the Eucharist makes the Church.* It makes of it an inner reality. By its hidden power, the members of the body come to unite themselves by becoming more fully members of Christ, and their unity with one another is part and parcel of their unity with the one single Head" (*Corpus Mysticum*, 88; emphasis added). For a very instructive study that brings Henri de Lubac's Eucharistic ecclesiology into an illuminating ecumenical dialogue with the Greek Orthodox theologian John Zizioulas, see Paul McPartlan, *The Eucharist Makes the Church: Henri de Lubac and John Zizioulas in Dialogue* (Edinburgh: T and T Clark, 1993). One has only to read the work of Yves Congar, OP, in order to realize that this kind of dialogue takes place not beyond but very much within the fundamental theological parameters set by Thomas's (patristically inspired) Christ-centered Eucharistic theology.

157. De Lubac, *Corpus Mysticum*, 251.

158. Scheeben, *The Mysteries of Christianity*.

159. Ibid., 500.

160. Pope John Paul II, in *Ecclesia de Eucharistia*, seems to reemphasize and enlarge a theme present already in Pius XII's encyclical *Mediator Dei*: "It is on this doctrinal basis that the cult of adoring the Eucharist was founded and gradually developed as something distinct from the sacrifice of the Mass. The reservation of the sacred species for the sick and those in danger of death introduced the praiseworthy custom of adoring the blessed Sacrament which is reserved in our churches. This practice of adoration, in fact, is based on strong and solid reasons. For the Eucharist is at once a sacrifice and a sacrament; but it differs from the other sacraments in this, that it not only produces grace, but contains in a permanent manner the Author of grace Himself. When, therefore, the Church bids us adore Christ hidden behind the eucharistic veils and pray to Him for spiritual and temporal favors, of which we ever stand in need, she manifests living faith in her divine Spouse who is present beneath these veils, she professes her gratitude to Him and she enjoys the intimacy of His friendship" (*Mediator Dei*, par. 131).

APPENDIXES

161. *Opera omnia iussu Leonis XIII P.M. edita*, vol. 40 (Rome: Ad Sanctae Sabinae, 1968).

162. Denzinger, no. 802 (267).

163. On this topic, see the informative study by Ulrich Horst, OP, *The Do-minicans and the Pope: Papal Teaching Authority in the Medieval and Early Modern Thomist Tradition*, trans. James D. Mixson (Notre Dame, Ind.: University of Notre Dame Press, 2006).

164. Yves Congar, OP, "Saint Thomas Aquinas and the Infallibility of the Papal Magisterium," *The Thomist* 38, no. 1 (1974): 81–105, at 93.

165. Brock, "St. Thomas and the Eucharistic Conversion," 535–36, at 536.

166. Herbert McCabe, OP, *God Still Matters*, ed. Brian Davies, OP (London: Continuum, 2002), 115.

167. See also more recently among similar lines the instructive article by Horst Seidl, "Sul concetto di sostanza nel dogma tridentino della transustanziazione. Commenti metafisici a discussioni attuali," *Aquinas* 41, no. 2 (1998): 223–40.

168. Schillebeeckx, *The Eucharist* (New York: Sheed and Ward, 1968), 53–66.

169. A slightly more sophisticated version of this question—but one displaying remarkable deficiencies of understanding regarding Aristotle's categories, theory of language, and physics—can be found in Ian Robinson, "Thomas Cranmer on the Real Presence," *Faith and Worship* 43 (1997): 2–10.

170. *On Sophistical Refutations* 2, 165b3, quoted in *ST* II-II, q. 2, a. 3, co.

Selected Bibliography

—— : ——

WORKS BY THOMAS AQUINAS

De malo. Edited by P. Bazzi and P. M. Pession. In *Quaestiones disputatae,* vol. 2, edited by Raymund M. Spiazzi, OP. Rome: Marietti, 1965.

De potentia Dei. Edited by P. M. Pession. In *Quaestiones disputatae,* vol. 1, edited by Raymund M. Spiazzi, OP. Rome: Marietti, 1965.

De principiis naturae ad Fratrem Sylvestrum. In *Opuscula Philosophica,* edited by Raymund M. Spiazzi, OP. Rome: Marietti, 1954.

Expositio super primam et secundam Decretalem ad archidiaconum Tudertinum. In *Opera omnia iussu Leonis XIII P.M. edita,* vol. 40. Rome: Ad Sanctae Sabinae, 1968.

In Aristotelis librum de anima commentarium. Edited by Angelus M. Pirotta, OP. Rome: Marietti, 1959.

In duodecim libros Metaphysicorum Aristotelis expositio. Edited by M. R. Cathala, OP, and R. M. Spiazzi, OP. Rome: Marietti, 1964.

In librum beati Dionysii de divinis nominibus expositio. Edited by Ceslaus Pera, OP. Rome: Marietti, 1950.

In octo libros Physicorum Aristotelis expositio. Edited by P. M. Maggiòlo, OP. Rome: Marietti, 1954.

Quaestiones quodlibetales. Edited by Raymund M. Spiazzi, OP. Rome: Marietti, 1949.

Summa contra Gentiles. Sancti Thomae Aquinatis Doctoris Angelici Opera Omnia iussu edita Leonis XIII P.M., vols. XIII–XV. Rome: Commissio Leonina, 1918–30.

Summa contra Gentiles. Liber de veritate catholicae fidei contra errores infidelium seu "Summa contra gentiles." 4 vols. Edited by Ceslaus Pera, OP, Petrus Marc, OSB, and Petrus Caramello. Rome: Marietti, 1963.

Summa Theologiae. 3rd ed. Turin: Edizioni San Paolo, 1999.

TRANSLATIONS OF WORKS BY THOMAS AQUINAS

The Aquinas Prayer Book: The Prayers and Hymns of St. Thomas Aquinas. Edited and translated by Robert Anderson and Johann Moser. Manchester, N.H.: Sophia Institute Press, 2000.

Commentary on Aristotle's De Anima. Translated by Kenelm Foster and Sylvester Humphries. Revised edition. Notre Dame, Ind.: Dumb Ox Books, 1994.

Commentary on Aristotle's Metaphysics. Translated by John P. Rowan. Notre Dame, Ind.: Dumb Ox Books, 1995.

Commentary on Aristotle's Physics. Translated by Richard J. Blackwell, Richard J. Spath, and W. Edmund Thirlkel. Notre Dame, Ind.: Dumb Ox Books, 1999.

The De Malo of Thomas Aquinas. Latin-English. Edited by Brian Davies, OP. Translated by Richard J. Regan. Oxford: Oxford University Press, 2001.

On the Power of God (Quaestiones disputatae de potentia Dei). Translated by the English Dominican Fathers. Westminster, Md.: Newman Press, 1952.

Summa contra Gentiles, Book Four: Salvation. Translated with an introduction and notes by Charles O'Neil. Notre Dame, Ind.: University of Notre Dame Press, 1975.

Summa Theologiae. Translated by the Fathers of the English Dominican Province. New York: Benziger Bros., 1948.

Summa Theologica, vol. 30: *Das Geheimnis der Eucharistie.* Deutsch-Lateinische Ausgabe (Die Deutsche Thomas-Ausgabe). Commentary by Damasus Winzen, OSB. Salzburg: Verlag Anton Pustet, 1938.

THOMIST COMMENTATORS AND CLASSICAL THOMIST INTERPRETERS

Bobik, Joseph. *Aquinas on Being and Essence: A Translation and Interpretation.* Notre Dame, Ind.: University of Notre Dame Press, 1965.

————. *Aquinas on Matter and Form and the Elements: A Translation and Interpretation of the* De Principiis Naturae *and the* De Mixtione Elementorum *of St. Thomas Aquinas.* Notre Dame, Ind.: University of Notre Dame Press, 1998.

Billot, Louis, SJ. *De ecclesiae sacramentis: Commentarius in tertiam partem S. Thomae.* Rome: Ex typ. Pontificia Instituti Pii IX, 1914.

Cajetan, Tommaso de Vio Gaetani, OP. *Commentaria in Summam Theologiae Sancti Thomae Aquinatis (1507–1522).* In *Sancti Thomae Aquinatis Doctoris Angelici Opera Omnia iussu impensaque Leonis XIII P.M edita,* vols. 4–12. Rome: Leonine Commission, 1886–1906.

Doronzo, Emmanuel, OMI. *Tractatus dogmaticus de eucharistia,* vol. 1: *De sacramento.* Milwaukee, Wis.: Bruce Publishing, 1947.

Garrigou-Lagrange, Réginald, OP. *De Eucharistia accedunt De Paenitentia quaestiones dogmaticae Commentarius in Summam theologicam S. Thomae.* Rome: Marietti, 1943.

Gredt, Joseph, OSB. *Logica: Philosophia Naturalis*. Freiburg: Herder, 1956.

John of St. Thomas, OP. *Cursus philosophicus thomisticus secundum exactam, veram, genuinam Aristotelis et Doctoris Angelici mentem*. 3 vols. Paris: Vivès, 1883.

Sylvester of Ferrara, Francis, OP. *Commentaria in libros quatuor contra gentiles sancti Thomae de Aquino*. In *Sancti Thomae Aquinatis Doctoris Angelici Opera Omnia iussu edita Leonis XIII P.M.*, vols. XIII–XV. Rome: Commissio Leonina, 1918–26.

PAPAL, CONCILIAR, AND MAGISTERIALLY INVITED DOCUMENTS, AS WELL AS PAPAL WRITINGS

All papal pronouncements from Leo XIII onward can be found online at vatican. va or papalencyclicals.net.

Benedict XVI, Pope. *Sacramentum Caritatis*. Apostolic Exhortation. February 22, 2007.

Catechism of the Catholic Church. Second Edition Revised in Accordance with the Official Latin Text Promulgated by Pope John Paul II. Vatican City: Libreria Editrice Vaticana, 1997.

Decrees of the Ecumenical Councils. 2 vols. Edited by Norman P. Tanner, SJ. London / Washington, D.C.: Sheed and Ward / Georgetown University Press, 1990.

Denzinger, Heinrich. *Enchiridion symbolorum definitionum et declarationum de rebus fidei et morum. Kompendium der Glaubensbekenntnisse und kirchlichen Lehrentscheidungen*, Lateinisch-Deutsch. Edited by Peter Hünermann. 40th ed. Freiburg: Herder, 2005.

———. *Compendium of Creeds, Definitions, and Declarations on Matters of Faith and Morals*. Latin-English. Revised, enlarged, and, in collaboration with Helmut Hoping, edited by Peter Hünermann and edited by Robert Fastiggi and Anne Englund Nash for the English edition. 43rd ed. San Francisco: Ignatius Press, 2012.

International Theological Commission. "The Interpretation of Dogma." 1989.

John Paul II, Pope. *Fides et Ratio*. Encyclical Letter. September 14, 1998.

———. *Ecclesia de Eucharistia*. Encyclical Letter. April 17, 2003.

Leo XIII, Pope. *Mirae Caritatis*. Encyclical Letter. May 28, 1902.

Paul VI, Pope. *Mysterium Fidei*. Encyclical Letter. September 3, 1965.

Pius X, Pope. *Ad Diem Illum Laetissimum*. Encyclical Letter. February 2, 1904.

Pius XII, Pope. *Mediator Dei*. Encyclical Letter. November 20, 1947.

———. *Munificentissimus Deus*. Apostolic Constitution. November 1, 1950.

GENERAL

Adams, Marilyn McCord. *Some Later Medieval Theories of the Eucharist: Thomas Aquinas, Giles of Rome, Duns Scotus, and William Ockham*. Oxford: Oxford University Press, 2010.

Aristotle. *Categories. On Interpretation. Prior Analytics.* Translated by H. P. Cooke and Hugh Tredennick. Loeb Classical Library 325. Cambridge, Mass.: Harvard University Press, 1938.

———. *Metaphysics Books X–XIV. Oeconomica. Magna Moralia.* Translated by Hugh Tredennick and C. Cyril Armstrong. Loeb Classical Library 28. Cambridge, Mass.: Harvard University Press, 1935.

———. *Physics, Volume I: Books 1–4.* Translated by P. H. Wicksteed and F. M. Cornford. Loeb Classical Library 228. Cambridge, Mass.: Harvard University Press, 1957.

———. *Physics, Volume II: Books 5–8.* Translated by P. H. Wicksteed and F. M. Cornford. Loeb Classical Library 255. Cambridge, Mass.: Harvard University Press, 1934.

Armogathe, Jean-Robert. *Theologia Cartesiana: L'explication physique de l'Eucharistie chez Descartes et dom Desgabets.* The Hague: Nijhoff, 1977.

———. "Cartesian Physics and the Eucharist in the Documents of the Holy Office and the Roman Index (1671.6)." In *Receptions of Descartes: Cartesianism and Anti-Cartesianism in Early Modern Europe,* edited by Tad M. Schmaltz, 149–70. New York: Routledge, 2005.

Bauerschmidt, Frederick Christian. "That the Faithful Become the Temple of God." In *Reading John with St. Thomas Aquinas: Theological Exegesis and Speculative Theology,* edited by Michael Dauphinais and Matthew Levering, 293–311. Washington, D.C.: The Catholic University of America Press, 2005.

Bernadot, M. V., OP. *From Holy Communion to the Blessed Trinity.* Translated by Dom Francis Izard, OSB. Westminster, Md.: Newman Press, 1952.

Bobik, Joseph. "Dimensions of the Individuation of Bodily Substances." *Philosophical Studies* 4 (1954): 60–79.

Bonino, Serge-Thomas, OP, ed. "Saint Thomas et l'Onto-théologie." *Revue Thomiste* 95, no. 1 (1995): 5–192.

Bouëssé, Humbert, OP. "La causalité efficiente instrumentale de l'humanité du Christ et des sacrements chrétiens." *Revue Thomiste* 39 (1934): 33–57.

Brock, Stephen. "St. Thomas and the Eucharistic Conversion." *The Thomist* 65, no. 4 (2001): 529–65.

Brown, Christopher M. "Artifacts, Substances, and Transubstantiation: Solving a Puzzle for Aquinas's Views." *The Thomist* 71, no. 1 (2007): 89–112.

Buescher, Gabriel, OFM. *The Eucharistic Teaching of William Ockham.* St. Bonaventure, N.Y.: The Franciscan Institute, 1950.

Burr, David. "Quantity and Eucharistic Presence: The Debate from Olivi through Ockham." *Collectanea Franciscana* 44 (1974): 5–44.

Caputo, John D. *Heidegger and Aquinas: An Essay on Overcoming Metaphysics.* New York: Fordham University Press, 1982.

Chadwick, Henry. "Ego Berengarius." *Journal of Theological Studies* 40, no. 2 (1989): 414–45.

Chauvet, Louis-Marie. *Symbol and Sacrament: A Sacramental Reinterpretation of*

Christian Existence. Translated by Patrick Madigan, SJ, and Madeleine Beaumont. Collegeville, Minn.: Liturgical Press, 1995.

Cipolla, Richard G. "Selvaggi Revisited: Transubstantiation and Contemporary Science." *Theological Studies* 35, no. 4 (1974): 667–91.

Clark, Joseph T., SJ. "Physics, Philosophy, Transubstantiation, Theology." *Theological Studies* 12 (1951): 24–51.

Congar, Yves, OP. "The Idea of the Church in St. Thomas Aquinas." *The Thomist* 1, no. 3 (1939): 331–59. Reprinted with revisions in Yves Congar, OP, *The Mystery of the Church*, translated by A. V. Littledale, 53–74. Baltimore, Md.: Helicon Press, 1960.

———. "Saint Thomas Aquinas and the Infallibility of the Papal Magisterium." *The Thomist* 38, no. 1 (1974): 81–105.

Descartes, René. *The Philosophical Writings of Descartes*, vol. 1: *Principles of Philosophy*. Translated by John Cottingham, Robert Stoothoff, and Dugald Murdoch. Cambridge: Cambridge University Press, 1985.

Dewan, Lawrence, OP. "The Importance of Substance." In his *Form and Being: Studies in Thomistic Metaphysics*, 96–130. Washington, D.C.: The Catholic University of America Press, 2006.

Elders, Leo J., SVD. *Die Naturphilosophie des Thomas von Aquin*. Weilheim-Bierbronnen: Gustav-Siewerth-Akademie, 2004.

Feiner, Johannes, and Magnus Löhrer, eds. *Mysterium salutis: Grundriß heilsgeschichtlicher Dogmatik*. 5 vols. Einsiedeln: Benziger, 1965–76.

Floucat, Yves. *Pour une métaphysique de l'être en son analogie: Heidegger et Thomas d'Aquin*. Paris: Artège Lethielleux, 2016.

Garrigou-Lagrange, Réginald, OP. *The Sense of Mystery: Clarity and Obscurity in the Intellectual Life*. Translated by Matthew K. Minerd. Steubenville, Ohio: Emmaus Academic, 2017.

Geiselmann, Josef. *Die Eucharistielehre der Vorscholastiker*. Paderborn: Schöningh, 1926.

Grandi, Marcello de. "La sostanza del pane e del vino e la transustanziazione eucaristica (Ipotesi di lavoro)." *Divus Thomas* 106, no. 3 (2003): 163–96.

Gutwenger, Engelbert, SJ. "Substanz und Akzidenz in der Eucharistielehre." *Zeitschrift für katholische Theologie* 83 (1961): 257–306.

Harnack, Adolf von. *Lehrbuch der Dogmengeschichte*. 3 vols. Freiburg: Mohr, 1887–90.

———. *What Is Christianity?* Translated by Thomas Bailey Saunders. New York: Putnam, 1901.

Hart, David Bentley. "The Offering of Names: Metaphysics, Nihilism, and Analogy." In his *The Hidden and the Manifest: Essays in Theology and Metaphysics*, 1–44. Grand Rapids, Mich.: Eerdmans, 2017.

Heidegger, Martin. "The Onto-theo-logical Constitution of Metaphysics." In *Identity and Difference*, translated by Joan Stambaugh, 42–74. New York: Harper and Row, 1969.

Hibbs, Thomas S. *Dialectic and Narrative in Aquinas: An Interpretation of the* Summa contra gentiles. Notre Dame, Ind.: University of Notre Dame Press, 1995.

Horst, Ulrich, OP. *The Dominicans and the Pope: Papal Teaching Authority in the Medieval and Early Modern Thomist Tradition.* Translated by James D. Mixson. Foreword by Thomas Prügl. Notre Dame, Ind.: University of Notre Dame Press, 2006.

Humbrecht, Thierry-Dominique, OP. "L'eucharistie, 'représentation' du sacrifice du Christ selon Saint Thomas." *Revue Thomiste* 98, no. 3 (1998): 355–86.

Hütter, Reinhard. *Suffering Divine Things: Theology as Church Practice.* Translated by Doug Stott. Grand Rapids, Mich.: Eerdmans, 1999.

———. *Bound for Beatitude: A Thomistic Study in Eschatology and Ethics.* Washington, D.C.: The Catholic University of America Press, 2019.

Iserloh, Erwin. *Gnade und Eucharistie in der philosophischen Theologie des Wilhelm von Ockham: Ihre Bedeutung für die Ursachen der Reformation.* Steiner: Wiesbaden, 1956.

Jorissen, Hans. *Die Entfaltung der Transsubstantiationslehre bis zum Beginn der Hochscholastik.* Münster: Aschendorff, 1965.

———. *Der Beitrag Alberts des Großen zur theologischen Rezeption des Aristoteles am Beispiel der Transsubstantiationslehre.* Münster: Aschendorff, 2002.

Journet, Charles Cardinal. *The Mass: The Presence of the Sacrifice of the Cross.* Translated by Fr. Victor Szczurek, O. Praem. South Bend, Ind.: St. Augustine's Press, 2008.

La Soujeole, Benoît-Dominique de, OP. "The Importance of the Definition of Sacraments as Signs." In *Ressourcement Thomism: Sacred Doctrine, the Sacraments, and the Moral Life,* edited by Reinhard Hütter and Matthew Levering, 127–35. Washington, D.C.: The Catholic University of America Press, 2010.

———. *Introduction to the Mystery of the Church.* Translated by Michael J. Miller. Washington, D.C.: The Catholic University of America Press, 2014.

Langevin, Dominic, OP. *From Passion to Paschal Mystery: A Recent Magisterial Development Concerning the Christological Foundation of the Sacraments.* Fribourg: Academic Press Fribourg, 2015.

Leff, Gordon. *William of Ockham: The Metamorphosis of Scholastic Discourse.* Totowa, N.J.: Rowman and Littlefield, 1975.

Link, Wilhelm. *Das Ringen Luthers um die Freiheit der Theologie von der Philosophie.* 2nd ed. Munich: Kaiser, 1955.

Lubac, Henri de. *Catholicism: Christ and the Common Destiny of Man.* Translated by Lancelot C. Sheppard and Sister Elizabeth Englund, OCD. San Francisco: Ignatius Press, 1988.

———. *Corpus Mysticum: The Eucharist and the Church in the Middle Ages.* Edited by Laurence Paul Hemming and Susan Frank Parsons. Translated by Gemma Simmonds, CJ, with Richard Price and Christopher Stephens. Notre Dame, Ind.: University of Notre Dame Press, 2006.

MacIntyre, Alasdair. "The End of Education: The Fragmentation of the American University." *Commonweal* (October 20, 2006): 10–14.

Maritain, Jacques. "La philosophie et l'unité des sciences." In his *Quatre essais sur l'esprit dans sa condition charnelle*, 227–56. Revised and expanded edition. Paris: Alsatia, 1956.

Marshall, Bruce D. "Identity, Being, and Eucharist." *The Saint Anselm Journal* 9, no. 2 (2014): 1–22.

McCabe, Herbert, OP. *God Still Matters*. Edited by Brian Davies, OP. London: Continuum, 2002.

McGuiness, Brian, ed. *Wittgenstein and the Vienna Circle: Conversations Recorded by Friedrich Waismann*. Oxford: Blackwell, 1979.

McInerny, Ralph. *Praeambula Fidei: Thomism and the God of the Philosophers*. Washington, D.C.: The Catholic University of America Press, 2006.

McPartlan, Paul. *The Eucharist Makes the Church: Henri de Lubac and John Zizioulas in Dialogue*. Edinburgh: T and T Clark, 1993.

Meyer, Hans. *Martin Heidegger und Thomas von Aquin*. Munich: Schöningh, 1964.

Moltmann, Jürgen. "Ökumene im Zeitalter der Globalisierung. Die Enzyklika 'Ut Unum Sint' in evangelischer Sicht." In *Ökumene—wohin? Bischöfe und Theologen entwickeln Perspektiven*, edited by Bernd Jochen Hilberath and Jürgen Moltmann, 87–97. Tübingen: Francke, 2000.

Nichtweiss, Barbara. *Erik Peterson: Neue Sicht auf Leben und Werk*. Freiburg: Herder, 1992.

O'Callaghan, John P. *Thomist Realism and the Linguistic Turn: Toward a More Perfect Form of Existence*. Notre Dame, Ind.: University of Notre Dame Press, 2003.

O'Meara, Thomas F., OP. "Theology of the Church." In *The Theology of Thomas Aquinas*, edited by Rik van Nieuwenhove and Joseph Wawrykow, 303–25. Notre Dame, Ind.: University of Notre Dame Press, 2005.

Peterson, Erik. *Ausgewählte Schriften*, vol. 1: *Theologische Traktate*. Würzburg: Echter, 1994. English translation: *Theological Tractates*. Edited and translated by Michael J. Hollerich. Stanford, Calif.: Stanford University Press, 2011.

Rahner, Karl. *The Shape of the Church To Come*. Translated and introduced by Edward Quinn. New York: Seabury, 1974.

Ratzinger, Joseph. "Das Problem der Transsubstantiation und die Frage nach dem Sinn der Eucharistie." *Theologische Quartalschrift* 147 (1967): 129–59.

Robinson, Ian. "Thomas Cranmer on the Real Presence." *Faith and Worship* 43 (1997): 2–10.

Rosier-Catach, Irène. *La parole efficace: Signe, rituel, sacré*. Paris: Éditions du Seuil, 2004.

Sabra, George. *Thomas Aquinas' Vision of the Church: Fundamentals of an Ecumenical Ecclesiology*. Mainz: Grünewald, 1987.

Scheeben, Matthias Joseph. *The Mysteries of Christianity*. Translated by Cyril Vollert, SJ. St. Louis, Mo.: Herder, 1951.

Schillebeeckx, Edward, OP. *The Eucharist*. Translated by N. D. Smith. New York: Sheed and Ward, 1968.

Schmaltz, Tad M. *Radical Cartesianism: The French Reception of Descartes.* Cambridge: Cambridge University Press, 2002.

Seckler, Max. *Das Heil in der Geschichte: Geschichtstheologisches Denken bei Thomas von Aquin.* Munich: Kösel, 1964.

Sedlmayr, Petrus, OSB. "Die Lehre des hl. Thomas von den *accidentia sine subjecto remanentia*—untersucht auf ihren Einklang mit der aristotelischen Philosophie." *Freiburger Zeitschrift für Philosophie und Theologie* 12 (1934): 315–26.

Seidl, Horst. "Zum Substanzbegriff der katholischen Transsubstantiationslehre: Erkenntnistheoretische und metaphysische Erörterungen." *Forum Katholische Theologie* 11 (1995): 1–16.

———. "Sul concetto di sostanza nel dogma tridentino della transustanziazione. Commenti metafisici a discussioni attuali." *Aquinas* 41, no. 2 (1998): 223–40.

Siewert, Gustav. *Das Schicksal der Metaphysik von Thomas zu Heidegger.* 3rd ed. Freiburg: Johannes Verlag Einsiedeln, 2006.

te Velde, Rudi. *Aquinas on God: The 'Divine Science' of the Summa Theologiae.* Burlington, Vt.: Ashgate, 2006.

Torrell, Jean-Pierre, OP. *Saint Thomas Aquinas*, vol. 1: *The Person and His Work.* Translated by Robert Royal. Washington, D.C.: The Catholic University of America Press, 1996.

Tschipke, Theophil, OP. *Die Menschheit Christi als Heilsorgan der Gottheit unter besonderer Berücksichtigung der Lehre des heiligen Thomas von Aquin.* Freiburg: Herder, 1940. French translation: *L'humanité du Christ comme instrument de salut de la divinité.* Translated by Philibert Secrétan. Foreword by Benoît-Dominique de la Soujeole, OP. Fribourg: Academic Press, 2003.

Tück, Jan-Heiner. *A Gift of Presence: The Theology and Poetry of the Eucharist in Thomas Aquinas.* Translated by Scott G. Hefelfinger. Foreword by Bruce D. Marshall. Washington, D.C.: The Catholic University of America Press, 2018.

Veatch, Henry Babcock. *Two Logics: The Conflict Between Classical and Neo-Analytic Philosophy.* Evanston, Ill.: Northwestern University Press, 1969.

Vijgen, Jörgen. *The Status of Eucharistic Accidents "sine subiecto": An Historical Survey Up to Thomas Aquinas and Selected Reactions.* Berlin: Akademieverlag, 2013.

Vollert, Cyril, SJ. "The Eucharist: Controversy on Transubstantiation." *Theological Studies* 22 (1961): 391–425.

Vonier, Anscar, OSB. *A Key to the Doctrine of the Eucharist.* Bethesda, Md.: Zaccheus Press, 2003–4.

Wallace, William H., OP. "Thomism and Modern Science." *The Thomist* 32 (1968): 67–83.

———. *The Modeling of Nature: Philosophy of Science and Philosophy of Nature in Synthesis.* Washington, D.C.: The Catholic University of America Press, 1996.

Weinandy, Thomas G., OFM Cap. *Does God Suffer?* Notre Dame, Ind.: University of Notre Dame Press, 2000.

Wippel, John F. *The Metaphysical Thought of Thomas Aquinas: From Finite Being*

to Uncreated Being. Washington, D.C.: The Catholic University of America
  Press, 2000.
Wittgenstein, Ludwig. *The Blue and Brown Books.* Oxford: Blackwell, 1958.
———. *Philosophische Untersuchungen, Schriften.* Frankfurt: Suhrkamp, 1960.

RECOMMENDED READINGS

Bernadot, Marie Vincent, OP. *From the Eucharist to the Trinity.* Translated by
  Dom Francis Izard, OSB. Introduction by Sr. Maria of the Angels, OP. Prov-
  idence, R.I.: Cluny Media, 2016.
Journet, Charles Cardinal. *The Mass: The Presence of the Sacrifice of the Cross.*
  Translated by Fr. Victor Szczurek, O. Praem. Preface by Bishop Salvatore
  Cordileone. South Bend, Ind.: St. Augustine's Press, 2008.
Levering, Matthew, and Michael Dauphinais, eds. *Rediscovering Aquinas and the
  Sacraments: Studies in Sacramental Theology.* Chicago: Hillenbrand Books,
  2009.
Lynch, Reginald, OP. *The Cleansing of the Heart: The Sacraments as Instrumental
  Causes in the Thomistic Tradition.* Washington, D.C.: The Catholic University
  of America Press, 2017.
Nutt, Roger W. *General Principles of Sacramental Theology.* Washington, D.C.: The
  Catholic University of America Press, 2017.
O'Connor, James T. *The Hidden Manna: A Theology of the Eucharist.* 2nd ed. San
  Francisco: Ignatius Press, 2005.
O'Neill, Colman E., OP. *Sacramental Realism: A General Theory of the Sacraments.*
  Princeton, N.J.: Scepter Publishers, 1998.
———. *Meeting Christ in the Sacraments.* Revised and introduced by Romanus
  Cessario, OP. New York: Alba House, 2002.
Ratzinger, Joseph Cardinal/Pope Benedict XVI. *The Spirit of the Liturgy.* Translat-
  ed by John Saward. San Francisco: Ignatius Press, 2000.
Schneider, Athanasius. *Dominus est—It is the Lord! Reflections of a Bishop of Cen-
  tral Asia on Holy Communion.* Translated by the Reverend Nicholas L. Gre-
  goris. Pine Beach, N.J.: Newman House Press, 2008.
Sokolowski, Robert. *Eucharistic Presence: A Study in the Theology of Disclosure.*
  Washington, D.C.: The Catholic University of America Press, 1994.
———. "The Eucharist and Transubstantiation." In his *Christian Faith & Human
  Understanding: Studies on the Eucharist, Trinity, and the Human Person,* 95–112.
  Washington, D.C.: The Catholic University of America Press, 2006.
Tück, Jan-Heiner. *A Gift of Presence: The Theology and Poetry of the Eucharist in
  Thomas Aquinas.* Translated by Scott G. Hefelfinger. Foreword by Bruce D.
  Marshall. Washington, D.C.: The Catholic University of America Press, 2018.
Vonier, Anscar, OSB. *A Key to the Doctrine of the Eucharist.* Bethesda, Md.: Zac-
  cheus Press, 2003–4.

Index of Names

———— : ————

General Index

———— : ————

accidents, metaphysical notion of, 28, 31–33, 38–39, 43–45, 47, 49, 53, 62, 76–77, 91n55, 93n66, 102n105, 105n115; kinds of, 31–32
adoration, Eucharistic, 115n160
angels, 33, 50
Aristotle: categories of, 30–31; demise of philosophy of nature of, 28
artifacts, 33–37

beatific vision, 5
Berengar of Tours: Eucharistic spiritualism of, 58–59, 109nn125–26
body of Christ: in heaven, 40, 42, 51, 54; in multiple places, 53
bread and wine: as matter of sacrament, 59; species of as subsisting after consecration, 45, 52, 97n87, 102n106, 107n119; as substances or artifacts, 33–37, 94n74

Chalcedon, Council of, 78
Chalcedon, dogma of, 12
charity, theological virtue of, 5, 10–11, 67, 83n8
Chauvet, Louis-Marie: adoption of an event-ontology, 81n3
circumincession: of persons of the Trinity, 96n84
concomitance. *See* real concomitance
connaturality, 83n8
Constance, Council of, 76

consubstantiation, 25, 72
Corpus Christi, feast of, 17, 88n37, 88n39

deception. *See* transubstantiation
deification, 66
dimensive quantity, accident of, 28, 32, 37–39, 41–56, 94n76, 95n80, 97n87, 98n93, 102n106, 103n108, 106n118; essence of quantity as distinct from, 51; as first accident of material substance, 47, 50–51, 55, 94n76, 103n108; two formal effects of, 46, 50–53, 55, 102n106
dogma: on the enduring value of dogmatic definitions, 21–23, 25–26, 77–78; historical relativization of, 18, 25–26, 77–78, 89n47
Donum Veritatis (Congregation for the Doctrine of the Faith), 1
dynamic presence theories, 22–23

Ecclesia de Eucharistia (John Paul II), 2, 19–20, 23, 70
ecclesial realism: as connected with Eucharistic realism, 68–69
ecumenism, 3, 82n5
equivocal generation, 34
essence-existence distinction, 32
"the Eucharist makes the Church" (de Lubac), 68, 114n156

faith, theological virtue of, 5, 10–11, 14, 62–65, 67–68, 75, 111n138, 112n139,